LIFE IN THE STUDIO

DELANY & HER CIRCLE

Yale Center for British
Sir John Soane's
Yale University

OF BEAUTY GROWING
British Studio Pottery

ADAMSON
OTHE

YALL

FRANCES PALMER
LIFE IN THE STUDIO
INSPIRATION AND LESSONS ON CREATIVITY

FOREWORD BY DOMINIQUE BROWNING

ARTISAN | NEW YORK

Library of Congress Cataloging-in-Publication Data

Names: Palmer, Frances (potter), author. | Browning, Dominique, author of foreword
Title: Life in the studio / Frances Palmer.
Description: New York, NY : Artisan, a division of Workman Publishing Co.,
   Inc., 2020. | "Foreword by Dominique Browning" - CIP title page.
Identifiers: LCCN 2020002005 | ISBN 9781579659059 (hardcover)
Subjects: LCSH: Palmer, Frances (potter) | Potters—United States—Biography.
Classification: LCC NK4210.P32 A2 2020 | DDC 738.092 [B]—dc23
LC record available at https://lccn.loc.gov/2020002005

Design by Elizabeth Van Itallie

Artisan books are available at special discounts when purchased in bulk for premiums and sales promotions as well as for fund-raising or educational use. Special editions or book excerpts also can be created to specification. For details, contact the Special Sales Director at the address below, or send an email to specialmarkets@workman.com.

For speaking engagements, contact speakersbureau@workman.com.

Published by Artisan
A division of Workman Publishing Co., Inc.
225 Varick Street
New York, NY 10014-4381
artisanbooks.com

Artisan is a registered trademark of Workman Publishing Co., Inc.

Published simultaneously in Canada by Thomas Allen & Son, Limited

Printed in China

First printing, August 2020

10 9 8 7 6 5 4 3 2 1

TO MY FAMILY

Contents

10 Foreword by Dominique Browning

15 Introduction

16 PART I
Begin as You Mean to Go On

102 PART II
Routine Is Everything

178 PART III
Looking Forward

242 Sources

245 Further Reading

248 Acknowledgments

252 Index

Foreword

I first met Frances Palmer in the guise of a pot. A picture of a pot, actually, one in a beautiful series of photographs that was to be featured in a forthcoming issue of *House & Garden*, where I was editor in chief. It was a charming, jaunty, proud, distinctive vase, with a handle perched on a swollen, wide-wale-corduroy-striped belly and a pearly string of beads around its neck, its glossy cream hue vibrant against a saffron background. The vase was tall enough that the sunflowers crammed into it nodded out from the top. Gazing at pictures from the photo shoot, I knew instantly that the pot conveyed the essence of gardens, the joy of living with flowers, and the pleasure of summer's magic, and I asked the art director to mock it up into a cover for the magazine.

And, dear reader, I bought the pot. Of course.

Over the years, I saw Frances from time to time at various art, garden, and design events. Then, after *House & Garden* folded, she became a friend who helped me up out of the slough of despond into which I had pitched myself. We walked, we talked, we looked at art and listened to music. I learned a great deal about resilience and friendship—and beauty.

Since I acquired that first vase, I have assembled a treasured collection of Frances's work. It is instantly recognizable. Pieces slump, pout, pucker, wobble, fold; necks sport ruffs and beads; an entire

surface might be collaged with flowers molded from blossoms Frances brings in from the garden; sometimes the surface is a simple but vibrant glaze of oxblood or celadon or, my favorite these days, the mysterious, murky "tea dust" that does, indeed, look like a wash of the dregs from the bottom of a teacup, ready to reveal your fate. Her work is durable and strong, meant to be used every day. It feels contemporary, but it echoes ancient forms, especially those from China and Korea. She has a free and unrestrained hand but is also capable of the discipline and focus and centeredness that the potter's wheel demands. There's nothing pretentious about her work, or her; one needn't read catalog copy to understand what she is doing. Not for her, the intellectual-seeming discussions about "What is art, what is craft?" She doesn't want her pottery to be held at arm's length.

These are living works, and works for living. A small mug ("You know, I made that as a vase," Frances once remarked, quizzically) I use for a daily turmeric infusion has become stained in swirling shades of mustard and tobacco yellow. A bowl, dropped in the sink and broken into pieces, was restored, bright gold veins scarring the surface, using a Japanese art of repair (kintsugi) that Frances had learned. A cake plate whose rim is pierced and scalloped is the only way to share an olive oil cake I

A bookshelf in Dominique Browning's home is filled with collected treasures— seedpods, feathers, and a group of my pots: a black stoneware bowl and a shino-glazed porcelain pot, on the top shelf, and, on the bottom shelf, porcelain pots with oxblood, shino, and celadon glazes.

have made, because it is such a Very Big Deal when I bake that there must be commensurate drama in the presentation of my labor. But I feel that way about anything anyone makes: we go to such trouble, we should celebrate the bounty on our tables and the glory of our gardens on our most fabulous plates and platters. Frances makes the good stuff, and she always uses the good stuff—and urges us all to do so.

I think it is worth giving you a sense of the person whose wonderful work fills the pages of the book you hold. My mother, raising four children in Connecticut, used to scoff at the women in our town who wouldn't get off the tennis court, and anyway were too afraid to drive into New York City for a concert or an exhibit. She would have approved of Frances, who transformed the tennis court on the property she and her husband bought into a walled garden full of raised planting boxes, and is frequently on a train headed into the city from her Connecticut home, drawn in by an opera or an art show.

Those excursions are always fruitful. Frances has taught her friends a great deal about how to see, how to slow down enough to actually notice an interesting detail in an ancient vessel at the Met. I vividly recall a retrospective of the paintings of Agnes Martin at the Guggenheim; Frances had her notebook out, and she was sketching patterns and lines, taking notes. Months later, those sketches were transformed into patterned

clay tiles I used to cover the wall above my stove.

She has a gift for forging durable friendships; I have met women with whom she raised children, or even studied in college. Frances's friends are as gifted as she is: they keep chickens, teach cooking classes, knit sweaters, create precious pieces of jewelry. We all know she is someone to call at the crack of dawn when you can't sleep, because her day is long under way, and we know never to phone Frances after six p.m., when she is deranged with exhaustion.

Frances is adept at making new friends, too. The man who helps her raise bees. The woman who ships foraged weeds and grasses and clematis from California for photo shoots or the tutorials Frances holds on the art of flower arranging. She nurtures young photographers and artists, welcoming them to her studio, and to her table. She learns from everyone.

Lunch with Frances isn't a matter of power suits and posturing. It is a chance to sit with a fragrant bowl of soup that's been simmering on the stove for hours, talking over the day's political news. She'll send you home with a bowl of fresh granola or a jar of honey from her hives or a few slices of sourdough or an armful of dahlias from her garden. (She is never on trend; she started cultivating dahlias when garden snobs disdained their exuberant dazzle. Now, naturally, everyone's planting them.)

We all know that she will console— or tease—with a line from one of the many movies and books that she has memorized nearly in their entirety, having watched or read them dozens of times in rotation. Among her favorites are *Pride and Prejudice, Bleak House, Jane Eyre,* and *To Kill a Mockingbird*—but also *The Princess Bride* and *Legally Blonde,* which she assures me are classics of rich, joyful profundity. "I do tend to memorize the most benign and absurd things," she confesses. "I can't handle the deep and the dark." Certainly, Frances has faced dark times in her life, more than most people. They have forged in her a self-reliance, a sturdy sort of resilience. And a great appreciation for living.

Frances's life in the studio brims and spills over into her life in the kitchen, life at the table, life in the garden, life among friends and family—and this in turn is the essence of life in the studio, as you will see in these pages. Beauty is an indispensable part of this life. So, too, are humor and charm. And an embrace of the unexpected, the accidental. Frances cannot help herself: She "gives birth to beauty as if this were the natural thing to do," as the Japanese philosopher Sōetsu Yanagi wrote in *The Beauty of Everyday Things.* Frances lives with a kind of unconscious grace.

I have not sat at a potter's wheel to make a pot since I was in high school. I have never made a layer cake—though Frances has coached me through roasting a chicken. I'll never keep bees or grow dahlias. Yet in the pages of this, her first book, there are lessons for me, and for all of us. Lessons about how to live a life of curiosity, joy, pleasure, creativity, and playfulness. Lessons about paying attention. And, yes, lessons about gardening and baking. About what it takes to apply oneself to any sort of creative act—the determination and perseverance and productivity. The insouciance about failure, because, after all, it's about the life, not the product. Frances is invariably cheerful about the outcome of her efforts, and that should give us all heart.

She generously invites the reader into these pages and opens up her world to us so that we may partake of that beautiful grace every day. Keeping company with Frances's work and spirit enhances the comforts, the solace and the safety, we find at home. These are gifts.

To use her favorite send-off—a motto she's adopted from her beloved and hilarious *Princess Bride*—"Have fun storming the castle!"

—DOMINIQUE BROWNING
Cofounder and Director, Moms Clean Air Force
Associate Vice President, Environmental Defense Fund

Introduction

As of this writing, I have been a potter for more than thirty years. My husband, Wally, and I have lived in a colonial house from the 1850s for twenty-five of those years, along with our three children and numerous dogs and cats. Over time, Wally and I built a barn that now serves as my studio, with kilns inside and out. Adjacent to the studio, we designed and planted two cutting gardens: a large, round, fenced plot and a collection of thirty raised beds situated on an old tennis court.

I've had the good fortune and determination to craft a universe that supports my endeavors; the house, studio, and gardens blend together in my work. I've grown flowers to fill my pots, thinking that the blooms give context and proportion to the forms. I've tracked the light in the studio across the day and used my camera to experiment with how to best capture it. What goes on my platters and in my bowls and mugs is as important to me as what goes into producing them; I've whipped up innumerable meals in the kitchen to feed my family, and entertained friends and clients in both the house and the studio. It's all about living with the clay.

Underlying these efforts is unpredictability—of ceramics, of gardening, of cooking and baking—which I not only accept but happily embrace. I am endlessly fascinated by these processes and their results—all of which are ultimately out of my hands. I love the surprise that can come from a flower or a glaze and the joy in finding a delicious new recipe.

Over the years, I have met many people who yearn to be creative. They tell me how much they wish to have their own space in which to work. At some point, they say, they will leave their day-to-day lives behind and follow their inner voice. Yet it doesn't have to be an all-or-nothing proposition; I encourage anyone to find a balance that allows them to both support and express themselves. This book is my attempt to articulate the philosophies behind my practice so that they may encourage others to follow their own artistic paths.

I would not presume to say that my approach is the best or only way to forge a life in the studio, but it is one that has served me well. From an outside perspective, the results of my work may seem to emerge easily, but it requires discipline and perseverance to produce day in and day out. My craft has continued to evolve as I continue to push myself, learning much along the way. It is my hope that in distilling strategies developed over nearly three decades of creative pursuits, I will be able to offer insight anyone can adapt for their own imaginative adventures.

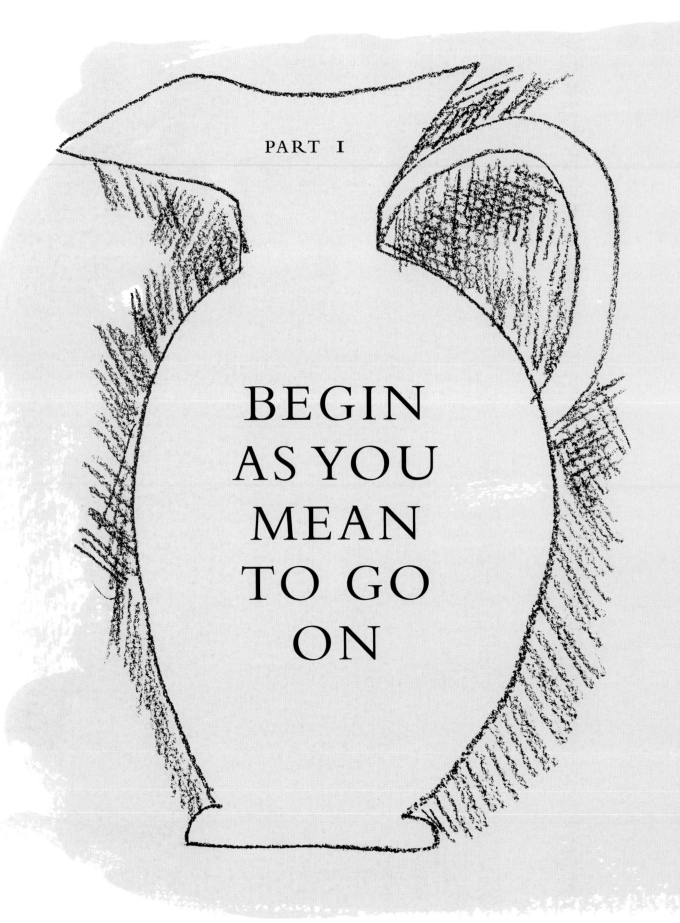

PART I

BEGIN
AS YOU
MEAN
TO GO
ON

When I began taking ceramics classes, I knew nothing about making pottery. I had worked in other media and had always been good with my hands, but the technical requirements of ceramics were new to me, and there was much to discover. It was as though I were Dorothy in *The Wizard of Oz*, setting out on the spiraling yellow brick road. But I didn't find this intimidating in the least; rather, I knew it was essential to be a beginner, to immerse myself in the process and allow myself time to gain experience through successes and failures.

Since then, my art has been an ongoing exploration and learning process, as I am mostly self-taught. This is also the way I have progressed as a gardener, cook, and photographer. It is the way I work best. It took time and patience to begin at the beginning, but I found myself in the middle before I realized it, and I've been moving forward ever since.

Practice Makes Purpose

Producing functional ceramics is central to my practice. When I sit at the wheel, I have an ongoing internal dialogue about the relationship between aesthetics and purpose. The earliest examples of ancient pottery combine these qualities in equal measure. Each piece tells a story about its creation, which imbues it with character. My hope is that my work, too, conveys much more than its intended purpose, and that it encourages constant use. I imagine that it never sits in one place for too long, and that as the pot moves from shelf to table and back again, it communicates an appreciation of life's moments, big and small.

The pots from antiquity that we admire today were originally used for all kinds of ceremonies and meals and not merely for display. I am grateful to be part of this time-honored tradition. A cup or vase is useful, yes, but also sculptural, as a result of being formed by hand. My clients understand that each piece is inherently imperfect, and they trust in the workmanship that accounts for its singular beauty. My hand is forever present, and a part of my spirit is carried with the vessel. I strive to embody graciousness in the making that will be evident in the pot as it becomes part of someone else's daily rituals.

Of course, I am not alone in this thinking. The Japanese writer Sōetsu Yanagi examines the idea of living with practical objects that add a sense of poetry to one's quotidian life in *The Beauty of Everyday Things*, a book I reference often. His words remind me that utility brings the work into a home: Its purpose is to be part of a timeless domestic routine. Recently, I read the poem "To Be of Use," by Marge Piercy, which sums up exactly how I consider the relationship between form and function, especially in its last lines:

> But the thing worth doing has a shape
>   that satisfies, clean and evident.
> Greek amphora for wine or oil,
> Hopi vases that held corn, are put in
>   museums
> but you know they were made to be
>   used.
> The pitcher cries for water to carry
> and a person for work that is real.

Since I began making ceramics, my family and I have been surrounded by my pots. Just as I cut flowers in the garden for arranging, I choose serving pieces I have produced for our table—plates, bowls, and mugs for daily meals, but also vessels for special occasions, like footed cake stands that hold birthday cakes year after year, and the oversized plate on which my daughter's wedding cake was displayed. These everyday and celebratory pieces reinforce my philosophy about making and its result, and about the fragility of time.

Opposite: This collection of glazed, wood-fired mugs was designed with the users' morning coffee or tea in mind. I love the textures and colors that resulted from the pots' exposure to the flame in different parts of the kiln. The darker pieces were thrown in brown stoneware and the lighter in translucent porcelain.

Following pages: My dear friend Phoebe Cole-Smith is an amazing chef and gardener. She has been collecting—and using—my pots for more than twenty-five years. It is wonderful to see how they live in her kitchen.

My Foundations in Art

From an early age, I wished to be an artist. At my request, I was given drawing classes, and my mother bought me any art books that I asked to read, which were many, as I was eager to study and learn everything I could. We often made the trip together from our home in New Jersey to the Metropolitan Museum of Art in New York City because I loved looking at the paintings and sculptures firsthand. I was especially captivated by art that is a process, meaning that the result is as dependent on the characteristics and opportunities of the medium as it is on the artist's intent. I was—and remain—intrigued by how work shifts and changes as it progresses in ways that have nothing to do with the individual, due to the nature of their craft.

I remember exactly how certain artworks impacted me—not only because I admired them aesthetically but because they sparked my curiosity. I was eager to understand how they came to be. *What materials were used to create that drawing, painting, sculpture, statue?* I wondered. *What techniques were employed, and what tools?* I am still just as interested in the *how* as in the *why* behind the work. I want to know what went into it, and to try to imagine myself similarly engaged. This exemplifies my lifelong obsession with the creative process.

While studying foreign service at Georgetown University, I took my first art history class and spent time wandering around the Smithsonian museums in Washington, DC. I felt a whole new world opening up around me. I decided to concentrate on art history and transferred to Barnard College in New York City. During my undergraduate years, I worked in the Columbia University art library and as a slide projectionist. The latter job enabled me to take all the art history and architecture classes I wanted (without having to pay for most of them). I loved every minute of this immersive study.

I went on to get a graduate degree in art history at Columbia, then took a job at the contemporary art space known as P.S. 1, in Long Island City, Queens. This was in the early 1980s, and many accomplished artists showed there at the beginning of their careers. My pay was low, but the work was fascinating. After about a year, I was put in charge of the sister gallery to P.S. 1, the Clocktower Gallery on Leonard Street in Lower Manhattan, and thereafter took a job at Petersburg Press, which published limited-edition prints by some of the greatest artists of the day. Being steeped in both the historic and contemporary art worlds provided a strong foundation for my future endeavors.

I was asked by Aerin Lauder to create a collection inspired by the Cycladic Islands of Greece to launch with her new fragrance, Aegea Blossom. The earthenware pieces shown here evoke Cycladic pottery from around 3000 to 2000 BC.

Finding My Calling

It was exciting to be surrounded by notable contemporary artists at Petersburg Press, but after a few years, I felt I needed to produce my own artwork rather than continue as an arts administrator.

I was spending many hours designing and making knitted garments while working full-time at the press, and in 1983, I decided to start my own knitwear company. I researched who could best help me scale up the production, and found the person who managed the knitwear collection for Perry Ellis. She worked with a team of freelance knitters out of an office in the Garment District in New York, and we collaborated to create a small line of sweaters. I began to sell to local stores, including Henri Bendel, Betsey Bunky Nini, and IF. Although I loved designing the sweaters, my operation was not sustainable at its small scale, and I grew frustrated trying to keep up with the seasonal demands of fashion. A mutual friend suggested that I meet with Wally Palmer, a successful designer for a menswear company who knew all about the knitwear business and could perhaps give me some pointers.

When we met, it was love at first sight. I never consulted with him about my business, and not long after our meeting, I realized that I was not interested in expanding my knitwear company. Wally and I married in 1986 and had a daughter shortly thereafter. We are still together—one daughter, two sons, and more than three decades later.

Before Wally and I began dating, he had purchased a modernist glass house in Weston, Connecticut, as a weekend place. We had an apartment in New York City's West Village and were going back and forth until our daughter, Daphne, was born, at which point we moved to Connecticut full-time.

It turned out I was completely unprepared for living in suburbia. Wally and I knew only one couple who lived nearby, and I had never held a baby in my life. No one back then talked about the challenges of nursing or postpartum depression, and I thought I had failed on every count. It was all a bit of a disaster, and if not for an amazing pediatrician who took Daphne and me under his wing, I'm not sure we both would have made it!

After this rocky start adjusting to motherhood and life in Connecticut, Wally suggested that I embark on something new, something I had always wanted to try but had never had time for. In that period, I was reading about the Omega Workshops, the artist compound of the Bloomsbury Group in early-twentieth-century England. I was fascinated by these artists who produced all the decorative aspects of their environment: paintings, fabric, wallpaper, pottery, and clothing that they lived with every day. I was intrigued by the idea of making my own pottery to use when entertaining. I signed up at the Silvermine Arts Center in New Canaan, Connecticut—a wonderful school that was started by local sculptors in 1908—and learned to throw.

Making ceramics appealed to me immediately. It was a natural extension of the things I loved to do: cook, entertain, and arrange flowers (although it would be years before I had a garden, I went often to the wholesale flower market on West Twenty-Eighth Street in New York City for a steady supply of fresh blooms). Now I would be able to set the table with plates, bowls, and vases I had made myself. My background in art history was a perfect complement to my newfound passion; I was able to study different periods and artists who produced work that I admired and translate these ideas into my own style of pottery.

After a year or so of throwing classes, I had grasped the essentials. I was not keen, however, on the stoneware (which effectively burned out any bright glaze colors) and 1960s-style-ceramics clays and glazes at the guild. My vision was to work with a white, low-fire clay that I could paint on, in a technique similar to that of the Omega Workshops pottery, so I bought a used wheel and kiln and set up my own home studio in the family room of our formerly pristine house!

Following pages:
A selection of my first painted stoneware and white earthenware pieces. I took much joy in thinking up the patterns and colors, and each design is one of a kind.

ON PERSEVERANCE

My mother was a very practical person, adept at many things. She taught me how to sew and knit, how to work with my hands. Our house was the location for most holidays and other celebrations, as she was the best cook in the extended family, and she generously and patiently showed me how to set a table, compose a meal, and bake (pies, especially).

A great athlete, my mother competed in tennis and golf. She was a master bridge player and often teamed up with my father to compete in tournaments. She also handled the accounts for my father's various businesses. With all of these activities inside and outside the home, my mother maximized her time with the utmost efficiency. I learned multitasking skills from her, as well as how to channel my energy productively—both of which serve me well to this day.

One lesson in particular stands out in my memory. I must have been around seven years old when my mother taught me the recipe for pie dough that I have used ever since. She put the flour and butter in a bowl and explained how to make a crumb before adding her secret ingredient, orange juice in place of water. When I attempted to pull the flour and butter together, for some reason the mixture became too wet. My mother calmly put that failed attempt aside and organized a fresh bowl. The texture of the crumb was much better the second time around, and when we added the orange juice, it all came together as it should.

The underlying lesson of my mother's pie-dough demonstration—to recognize that the first try may not succeed and that one needs to persevere—flows through all of my work. The goal is not perfection but rather an in-depth understanding of the process and appreciation of the journey.

GOAT CHEESE AND LEEK TART

This tart combines my mother's pie dough with a filling adapted from Alice Waters's *Chez Panisse Menu Cookbook*. (All of her books are well worn in my kitchen; I love the simple elegance of everything she does.) It's just the thing when I need to make something in the morning that can be left at room temperature until lunchtime.
Makes one 9-inch (23 cm) tart; serves 8

FOR THE DOUGH

1¼ cups (156 g) all-purpose flour, plus more
    if needed
2 tablespoons (25 g) sugar
Pinch of coarse salt
8 tablespoons (1 stick/113 g) unsalted butter,
    cubed, plus more for the pan
3 tablespoons (45 ml) orange juice, plus more
    if needed

FOR THE FILLING

8 tablespoons (1 stick/113 g) unsalted butter
3 to 4 pounds (1.3 to 1.8 kg) leeks (12 to
    14 small), white and light green parts only,
    washed well, trimmed, and julienned
Coarse salt and freshly ground black pepper
1 large egg
½ cup (120 ml) heavy cream
2 teaspoons Dijon mustard
Pinch of curry powder
4 ounces (113 g) fresh goat cheese
⅓ cup (38 g) bread crumbs

Preheat the oven to 400°F (205°C). Butter a 9-inch (23 cm) tart pan.

Make the dough: Whisk the flour, sugar, and salt in a large bowl. With a fork or pastry blender, cut the butter into the dry ingredients until the mixture is crumbly, with only pea-sized lumps remaining. Do not overwork. Pour in the juice and mix just to bring the dough together. It should not be wet or sticky, but you can add a bit more flour if it is. If the dough is too dry, add more juice, a tablespoon at a time. Form the dough into a ball or disc and set on a large sheet of waxed paper, and chill while you prepare the filling.

Make the filling: Melt 6 tablespoons (85 g) of the butter in a skillet, then cook the leeks over low heat, stirring, for 10 minutes. Season with salt and pepper, and let cool. Beat the egg lightly in a large bowl and stir in the cream, mustard, curry powder, salt, and pepper. Crumble in half of the cheese. Stir in the cooled leeks.

Prepare the tart: Roll the dough into a round a bit larger than the tart pan. Fit it into the pan, trimming or folding over any excess dough, and refrigerate for 15 minutes. Fill the shell with the leek mixture. Crumble the remaining cheese over the filling, then sprinkle with the bread crumbs. Melt the remaining 2 tablespoons (28 g) butter and drizzle over the top. Place the tart pan on a sheet pan and bake for 30 to 40 minutes, until the pastry is a beautiful brown. Transfer the tart pan to a wire rack to cool before unmolding and serving.

Being Centered

Learning to center the clay is the first step of throwing a pot and exemplifies my mantra "begin as you mean to go on" because this initial step is crucial to the outcome. If the lump will not center, you might as well pull it off the wheel and start over.

First, a measured weight of clay, wedged to remove air pockets and make it pliable, is placed on a bat (a flat, removable disk) or on the head of the potter's wheel. As the wheel begins to turn, a concentric circle emerges on the top of the clay to indicate the center. Hands are wetted with water from a nearby bucket, then placed on either side of the clay. With a bit of strength, the ball is moved into symmetry before the center opens and the sides pull up. There is a delicate balance between applying force and gently coaxing the clay into place as if it had a life of its own.

Often, I close my eyes as I begin centering and feel my way through this process with only my hands. I have to concentrate fully on what is happening at the wheel and allow the material to guide the result; extraneous thoughts must be put aside.

I love the calmness that centering requires. I need to approach the wheel in a tranquil frame of mind. The minute I experience stress or confusion, the clay senses it. The walls of the pot will come up unevenly, or the ball of clay might even swerve off the wheel. The shape will not take the form that I am intending if I do not begin correctly. If I feel tired or upset while at the wheel, I stop until I can pull myself together or I move on to another task; there is no point in trying to throw when my mind is unfocused.

In her iconic book *Centering in Pottery, Poetry, and the Person*, potter, poet, and essayist M. C. Richards states that centering "bears the future within it" and that it is "a space for ongoing development and differentiation." This extends beyond the wheel—for Richards, centering clay is a clear metaphor for finding purpose and self-understanding. Fundamentally, this is what I also experience when I begin to center the clay. It seems as though I am simply making a pot, yet the practice suggests a larger contemplation, and I feel joy that this is my task to accomplish.

Promotion and Patience

After my initial foray into pottery, I quickly realized how much I enjoyed working at the wheel and decided to find a way to sell my pots. I wanted to develop a business for three reasons: to approach the work with seriousness, to make functional pieces, and to earn my own income independent of my husband.

Since I did not study pottery at an art school, I did not have the advantage of receiving guidance from professors or other mentors. And though I believe there is artistry in what a potter creates, I wanted my pieces to feel approachable, not precious.

To begin, I analyzed the current market for functional pottery and decided I would prefer to sell my work in stores rather than through art galleries. (This was 1988, long before online retail was an option.) Galleries might mount one annual show of my pieces (at most), which would not move inventory quickly enough, nor would I be allowed the flexibility to find new outlets. Fortunately, a good friend with a shop in Westport, Connecticut, gave me an opportunity to sell my earliest pots. This allowed me to think of myself as a professional right from the start.

The best way to convince other design shops to carry my work was to get publicity. I started by writing directly to magazine editors. In this digital age, it's easy to forget how vital and powerful the magazine world was in the 1980s and the influence it exerted on consumers. I went to bookstores and searched for any magazines even remotely connected to design, scanning the mastheads and noting the names of the editors in chief, creative directors, and market editors. I wrote everyone on the list a letter and included photos of my pots. Little by little, editors reached out. Some visited my studio and wrote articles about the work. I believe they responded to the fact that I had contacted them personally. Even after my business had grown and I might have hired a publicist, I never did. I wasn't comfortable spending so much of my earnings on the services of an outside firm. More important, however, I've always felt that no one can represent the work as well as I do and that my personal approach is an integral part of my business.

Not every magazine mention resulted in sales, but the media attention gave me instant credibility. The articles undoubtedly contributed to the growth of my business, and they remain an important marketing tool. I became good friends with many of the editors, some of whom are now clients. These days, I don't have to do the same sort of legwork to get attention as I'm more often contacted directly for stories.

I relied on the same letter-writing strategy to approach retail stores. I sought out the best design arbiters around the country and reached out to them with photographs and magazine clips of my pots. Pottery in home stores seems commonplace now, but when I began, few potters were trying to sell through commercial venues. Eventually, the places I targeted—including Zona, an innovative shop on Greene Street in SoHo, and, later, Barneys New York—began to carry my work.

The best result of one of my "cold letters" came from the Japanese department store Takashimaya, the ultimate design destination in New York City from the 1990s until its closing in 2010. There was a flower shop on the first floor, designed by the brilliant French floral designer Christian Tortu. It was truly groundbreaking and incredibly chic, with the most beautiful flowers and tools such as Japanese garden scissors. I was thrilled to have my work sold there. The store hosted several events for me and even featured my bud vases in a large display in the windows that looked out on Fifth Avenue. I'll never forget that experience. Fast-forward to 2019, when

I was commissioned to make large vases for the windows at the new Fotografiska museum (see page 182), housed in a landmark six-story Renaissance revival building on Park Avenue South in Manhattan. It was equally exhilarating to see the display of my pots in this gorgeous space, and it struck me how promotion is a continuing exercise in patience.

I like to remind myself that, indeed, patience is the most important aspect of my do-it-yourself business strategy. My favorite saying is "Rome wasn't built in a day." I certainly had to be willing to wait quite a while for my marketing and retail goals to be realized, and yet I have to remain patient still.

Now I sell most of my work through my studio. I've scaled back my accounts to just a few retailers around the country. The associations with these well-respected shops—and with design editors and creative directors—are an indispensable part of my business education and undoubtedly have put me on the path to where I am today.

How to Make a Pot

I am often asked how long it takes to make a pot. There is no easy answer. Each piece has its own timetable, and I try to keep as many pieces going simultaneously as possible. The benefit of having my studio next to my house is that I can pay close attention to the work and monitor it easily.

First, I decide what clay body to use. This choice often comes from the client, or it may be determined by the desired shape. (Porcelain, earthenware, and terra-cotta each have a range of technical possibilities and limitations; for more on this, see page 50.)

The intended design will dictate whether the piece will be thrown on the wheel or hand built from separate parts that are joined together. (You can see examples of each approach on pages 76 and 90.)

Next, I determine the amount of clay to use, including the amount to add proportional to the rate of shrinkage. There is no standard formula for this. I check the information provided with the clay I am working with, then I estimate. Every clay is different, and I have to consider the time it will take for the pot shape to be formed, dried to the point where it can be trimmed, bisque fired, and finally glaze fired.

I make a sketch of each piece in my notebook before I sit down to the wheel so that I know where I am heading. Then I hold the form in my mind as I bring up the walls. After my first attempt, I note the amount of clay and the dimensions (when wet)—this allows me to keep track of the design for when I go to throw the shape again. When I receive an order, I make at least four of the same design to cover any casualties along the way. I need backup to get through the multiple stages of creating each handmade piece.

One of the first rules I learned about making pots is that clay has a memory: When you throw a pot, the shape that is created at the beginning is the shape that the clay will move toward as it dries. If you try to make adjustments to the design after it is thrown—say, to change the perimeter of a cup's edge— it will inevitably return to its initial form during the firing. Sometimes I think I have successfully altered a pot, then I open the kiln to see that it did just what it pleased. I am amused and mystified by this magical process.

I throw larger amounts of clay in the morning, when I have the most energy and concentration. Weather affects the throwing. If it is damp and humid, the clay will not rise well under my hands. In winter, I make a fire in my woodstove to dry out the studio air; in summer, I reluctantly turn on the air conditioner.

Some days the throwing is perfect, and I can make wonderful things. I call these my "Felix Felicis" days, a reference to a good-luck potion in *Harry Potter and the*

These three porcelain bisque vases were inspired by pottery in the Museum of the Alhambra in Granada, Spain. Because of the variation in thickness of these pots' walls, they each transformed differently during the firing. I love the tilt of the one on the far left.

Half-Blood Prince. If the sun is shining and the air is cool, I open the barn windows and doors and all is well in the world. Moments like these make me feel as if I have drunk Harry's potion, too.

The dried pieces are loaded into the electric kiln for the first firing, known as a bisque. Before beginning this process, it is critical to ensure that the pots are completely dry. If there is a deadline, I make the largest vessels first so that they have the most opportunity to dry before firing. Since it can be difficult to determine if the clay in a large pot is sufficiently dry, my strategy is to place it on top of the kiln as I am firing another group of pots, to let the heat of the kiln serve double duty. I do this several times until I think (or pray) that the pot is truly ready. In the drying stage, many things can go awry: The pot can crack or warp, and finishing touches like the pedestal, handles, or beading can separate from the body.

Earthenware and terra-cotta are bisque fired to 1950°F (1066°C). Porcelain is bisqued at a much lower temperature, 1650°F (900°C), just to get it to the point where it can be glazed for the gas- or wood-kiln firing.

After the initial firing, assuming the pot has remained intact, I glaze the pots. When working with earthenware, I most often use a transparent glaze that covers the natural color of the clay. For the high-fire porcelain or stoneware, I dip into any number of glaze buckets that I have in the studio. (For more on glazes, see page 66.) I have usually planned out before the bisque firing how each clay body will be finished. I often fire one pot two to four times, sometimes reglazing each time, sometimes not, until I am happy with the outcome.

When I design porcelain pots with cobalt painting, I draw the patterns with pencil directly onto the clear-glazed pots. The graphite will burn off in the kiln, and the cobalt lines will sink into the glaze and pot body during the firing. On the following pages are these same pots after the firing.

Left: A full load of raw porcelain and stoneware pieces in the electric kiln, ready for bisque firing. This is a precarious stage, as the pots have to be stacked delicately—the slightest pressure on the rims will cause them to crack.

Opposite: Opening the gas kiln is always a surprise. The vase on the top left had fallen to the side, splitting from its pedestal base. I had a good laugh and was grateful that it had not damaged its neighbors (the vase in front of it was already broken; I keep it on hand to fill in empty space in the kiln). The center bowl on the second shelf made a curtsy—it was the first pot sold out of this load!

ON SELF-RELIANCE

When I was fourteen years old and in my first weeks of high school, I went to wake up my sixteen-year-old brother for school and found him dead from a heroin overdose.

Apart from the births of my children, my brother's death has been the defining moment of my life. At the age of thirteen, he severely pulled hamstring muscles in his leg and was put on morphine. He became addicted and by sixteen was using all sorts of drugs. In the months preceding his overdose, he had been sent to a facility for two weeks, but in 1970, there wasn't a clear understanding of how long it takes to be rehabilitated. The night he died, we were both at a large picnic with friends. I saw him walk away with a group of unfamiliar men, and I was afraid he was scoring dope. When I found him in the morning, I knew exactly what had happened.

Consequently, my family fell apart. My two older brothers were off at college and disconnected from the home scene. My parents were devastated by guilt and grief. I was pretty much left to my own devices, and I quickly developed my existential motto: One goes through life essentially alone. And though I have a wonderful husband and three lovely children, I have learned to rely on myself and not look to others to help me accomplish my goals.

I feel no bitterness about that period and know that every family has its own share of difficulties (as Tolstoy wrote in *Anna Karenina*, "each unhappy family is unhappy in its own way"). I try not to dwell on the past.

My brother's death, I suspect, is at the root of my determination to follow my own path, in my work and in my life. I suppose this experience also taught me how to pick myself up and keep going. I knew instinctively that no one was going to come along to rescue me. One might think that sounds somber or dark or depressing, but I see it another way: This family tragedy gave me a deep sense of inner strength. It also afforded me an early insight into the fragility of life. The broken bowl opposite is a metaphor for this perspective; I used the Japanese technique of kintsugi to piece it back together with gold. Its character is altered, but it's just as precious as it was before it shattered.

Each day needs to be experienced and not taken for granted. It requires determination to be alive, to confront challenges and be present. I remember distinctly finding this quote from Benjamin Franklin not long after my brother's death: "Dost thou love life? Then do not squander time, for that is the stuff life is made of." It has remained in my mind ever since, as I strive to grasp every moment, forge ahead, and do my best.

Inspiration Is Everywhere

I can honestly say that I study ceramics every day. The history of clay fills my brain, and when I sit down at the wheel, ideas flow out through my fingers and are transformed into shapes and forms. Whatever I produce comes out looking distinctly my own, yet it's informed by the work of potters who inspire me. Examining and studying other artists brings me tremendous, unending joy.

I think about historical references continually. Studying them provides a solid foundation on which to build a body of original work. These pots' design and function are so perfectly intertwined, without a need for embellishment, that they really cannot be improved upon. Many of the greatest sculptors have found this approach fruitful. Constantin Brâncuşi, for example, referenced Cycladic artworks from the Bronze Age in his twentieth-century works. Alberto Giacometti studied the funerary statues of the Etruscans, as well as Egyptian artifacts found in the royal tombs. Auguste Rodin was obsessed with ancient statuary, and though he never visited Greece, he collected classical Greek pottery, then combined it with his own plaster maquettes. Pablo Picasso, a master ceramist, married his vast knowledge of art history with a pronounced sense of humor.

In my ongoing search for the perfect embodiment of a footed bowl or vase, I inevitably peruse books on ancient pottery. If I have the time, I revisit the Cycladic and Etruscan galleries at the Metropolitan Museum of Art in New York City. These pots are created simply, with wonderful handles. The proportion of the pedestals gives each pot drama. I head up to the second-floor mezzanine to say hello to the Greek and Roman pots in the overflow room, and I note the shapes again and again.

If I am making tulipieres (pots with multiple openings to hold tulips, or any flower for that matter), I reach for books on Delft and Wedgwood. The Dutch were especially masterful at creating intricate pots for their prized tulips, and I love the challenge of constructing my own versions (a few are shown on pages 53, 193, 200, and 204).

I also look to twentieth-century potters such as Lucie Rie, Shōji Hamada, and George Ohr. Rie and Hamada were contemporaries, and I am drawn to the clean lines of their forms as well as the unusual glazes they used to make each piece more complex. A brilliant thrower, Ohr created paper-thin earthenware vases in the most eccentric and fantastical forms. I glean something new each time I page through the exhibition catalogs of these potters.

I study the exquisite forms of traditional Chinese pottery and their myriad glazes as well. These pots are often symmetrically thrown, with the glaze meticulously applied.

Opposite: Interior designer Young Huh commissioned a series of large terra-cotta pots for a room's window alcoves. I referenced Etruscan forms, giving each piece oversized, fanciful handles, and filled the pots with massive geraniums, which gave the space ebullience.

Following pages: I have always carried notebooks with me. I use them to document anything and everything: a shape to throw, a recipe to make, a list of work to complete, exhibitions to recall, and so on. I have drawn innumerable pots over the decades in these journals, and refer to them in the studio.

pencil
vase

1. picasso vase
2. small bowls - sm.
3. bowl with holes   bowl w/ldes
4. tray with holes
5. med. cake plate
6. large cake plate
7. bud vase
8. low wide bowl
9. coffee cups
10. #3 urn
11. compote
12. flower urn

tapestries - fans and ceiling
map room - primitive paintings
lapis lazuli blue

marble tables - bottom black/white
top white/black - heavy legs

        Raphael murals
        sistine chapel
        St. Peters - Bernini
Pietà
Villa Borghese - chiuso
        for restoration
Palazzo venezia
sat in front of Vittoria Emmanuel

1. vase
2. 7 lb. bowl
3. cake plate
4. urn
5. flower holder

In contrast, Japanese pots may be earthier, less even, and hand built. If these Japanese works are wood fired, the surface is unpredictable due to the random dispersion of ash falling in the kiln. This technique has long fascinated me—so much so that I've recently set up my own wood kiln (see page 236).

Though seemingly different, there is an underlying commonality among all the references to which I am drawn: a respect for and careful attention to both form and function.

When I am at the wheel, thoughts of these masters float through my head. My mind lingers on the charm of a jaunty handle, for example, and I begin to feel how to make it mine. The challenge feeds my curiosity and creativity.

Clay Has Personality

I read Lewis Carroll's *Alice's Adventures in Wonderland* and *Through the Looking-Glass* as a child, and I continue to find in both books a reflection of the absurdity of life. In one of my favorite passages from *Through the Looking-Glass*, Humpty Dumpty tells Alice that he pays words extra wages for allowing him to get so much good use out of them. In my work, when I feel I have used a clay body to its utmost inherent qualities, I feel I am paying the clay its extra wages.

I work with three commercially sourced clays, primarily: white earthenware, terra-cotta, and high-fire translucent porcelain. Each has its own temperament and range of possibilities, and I take my cues from the material. For example, a cake plate is best made from earthenware, because this low-fire clay accommodates the cantilevered expanse of the plate over the pedestal. It may warp slightly but mostly keeps its shape. Because porcelain becomes molten at high temperatures, it would be inclined to slump so would not be advisable for a cake plate. I mostly use porcelain clay for bowls and vases. I often select terra-cotta for garden pots, glazed or unglazed. This porous clay has served this purpose for centuries, but it is also useful for vases to be displayed indoors and for serveware.

WHITE EARTHENWARE

Earthenware is categorized as low-fire clay, indicating the temperature range at which it matures—it is fired to about 1950°F (1066°C) in an oxidized atmosphere (generally an electric kiln). Even after the initial bisque (the first firing, which removes bonded water chemically found in the raw clay body), earthenware is still porous. Therefore, vessels that will hold liquid or food must be completely coated with a glaze to seal the pores and prevent moisture from moving inside the piece.

White earthenware is a formula originally developed in the mid-1800s in England. It was intended to be an accessibly priced tableware option for middle-class people, in contrast to the more expensive, soft-paste porcelain ware being manufactured for the upper classes. The most famous example of white earthenware was produced in 1779 by Josiah Wedgwood, who named it creamware (and founded the ceramics manufacturing company that still bears his name).

The ceramics of the Omega Workshops, the London art cooperative founded in 1913 (and the original inspiration for my pottery), were mostly white earthenware with a white tin glaze. The artists Vanessa Bell and Duncan Grant approached the surface of each piece as if it were a canvas, using ceramic colors painted on the surface of the glaze. The pots had a vibrancy and design that was patterned and whimsical, similar to the artists' painted works on canvas.

This grouping, from left to right, includes white earthenware, high-fire translucent porcelain, and terra-cotta. Each likes to be thrown and then finished in its own way. Earthenware is the best choice when creating vessels with multiple components, porcelain takes well to gorgeous glazes of all kinds, and the handsome roughness of terra-cotta can offset more formal shapes.

At left, a stack of earthenware cake plates demonstrates the clay's ability to maintain its shape across vast expanses (the bottom plate's diameter is 18 inches/45.5 cm). The earthenware tulipiere opposite consists of seven separate thrown pieces that were then combined. While the clay was soft, the body was flattened into an oval shape and fluted.

After spending time with earthenware, I learned that it had wonderful throwing and assembling qualities. Earthenware is happy to be squashed, pulled, and manipulated into multiple directions without complaint. It can be thrown in disparate parts and still put together with great enthusiasm. A tulipiere, for example, might be thrown in as many as fifteen parts. Sometimes, though not always, cracks in earthenware (which can appear during the drying phase, caused by uneven or too rapid heat) can be repaired.

Because of earthenware's versatility, I approach each pot with fresh zeal. The qualities of the clay generously allow for creative license. Earthenware comprises the majority of my orders, and I am continually developing new shapes and finishes. Whenever I draw a complex or fantastic tulipiere in my notebook and then form it in earthenware, I am reminded again of Humpty Dumpty paying his words extra for doing additional work.

TERRA-COTTA

Terra-cotta, or "baked earth," has been an important material in everyday life for thousands of years. One can follow terra-cotta pottery through just about every civilization to document its presence— and not just in the garden. This sturdy clay is perhaps the most primitive of those that I work with.

Terra-cotta matures at a similar temperature to earthenware, approximately 1950°F (1066°C), yet it is grainier clay with a bit of grog, which I can feel in my fingers as I throw. (*Grog* refers to fired clay particles that range in size from fine to coarse; it is added to raw clay to reduce shrinkage.) Terra-cotta is not as forgiving as white earthenware clay. If a terra-cotta piece requires assembly, such as attaching a pedestal to the main body, I watch carefully for the perfect moment of dryness to connect the different parts. Should terra-cotta crack as it dries, it is difficult to repair.

Several years ago, I researched the history of terra-cotta for a lecture I gave to the Manhattan chapter of the North American Rock Garden Society. In the process, I discovered exquisite ancient pieces. One of my favorites is a drinking cup, or *skyphos*, from Crete that dates from the eleventh to ninth century BC. This flawlessly proportioned footed cup with handles is in the Metropolitan Museum of Art, as is a spectacular sixth-century Etruscan stand designed for vegetable and floral offerings. If you walk into the Egyptian gallery at the Met and take a right, there is a rough ware pot from southern Upper Egypt dating from 3900 to 3750 BC that looks so contemporary, it could be sitting in one of our gardens today. Terra-cotta was used to manufacture the first cuneiform writing tablets in Mesopotamia around 3100 to 2900 BC. The Cycladic civilization produced terra-cotta bowls from 3200 to 2800 BC; these have long served as my models for perfect simplicity of form.

My terra-cotta vessels range from classically footed and carved urns to vases with slumped walls. All the pieces here have been glazed in the interiors so that they can hold water.

To prepare for my lecture, I remade the ancient pots that I planned to discuss, as a way to understand the shapes more clearly. The forms are so beautiful that I was thrilled to have them represented in the studio. I consider this magnificent heritage each time I sit at the wheel.

I like to make terra-cotta pots that are unglazed on the outside and glazed on the inside so that they can be used as bowls or vases yet retain their raw outer surface. Happily, these pieces have recently come into fashion, and I've been getting more orders for these designs.

Most people do not understand the technical challenges of the material. I enjoy and respect terra-cotta enormously, however, and I love working with the clay.

HIGH-FIRE TRANSLUCENT PORCELAIN

The history of translucent porcelain is vast and complex. It mirrors the progress of technical advancement and trade over centuries originating in China and fanning out through Asia, then migrating to Europe.

It's a bit trickier to work with than earthenware or terra-cotta, however. Still, I yearned to throw this temperamental clay in order to produce the beautiful, classic celadon and oxblood glazes that are best achieved at high temperatures in the kiln. Each time I make a piece from porcelain, I understand better how to articulate my vision.

Unlike with earthenware, I try to fuss with the porcelain as little as possible after throwing. If a design requires the pot to be constructed in multiple parts and assembled, everything must be made at the same time, and I hover over the clay waiting for just the right moment, when the clay is at the ideal level of dampness,

to bring the pieces together. I try not to put pressure on the rims, and I handle the pots as gently as possible. The drying (which takes substantially longer than for white earthenware) cannot be rushed, or cracking will result. The pots must sit in the studio to dry at their own rate. The porcelain is first bisque fired at a low temperature (about 1650°F/900°C) to enable a bit more ease in handling for the glazing phase. Once the pots are ready for the glaze firing and carefully placed on the kiln shelves, the real magic begins.

I use a propane gas kiln for my porcelain pots, and to watch the temperature rise and the flames roll around the pots is endlessly thrilling. After approximately twelve hours, the kiln reaches about 2350°F (1288°C), at which point the porcelain vitrifies (transforms into a completely nonporous material, like glass). In theory, the clay does not need a glaze to seal its surfaces; the high-fire glazes simply add to the beauty of the piece.

For these pieces, I chose to exploit the cool, smooth white surface of bisque porcelain clay, leaving the pots unglazed. I was inspired by the simple forms of objects and cabinetry designed by the Shakers; I photographed the group together on a cherrywood "stage," alluding to the wood commonly used by these makers.

Here, porcelain and earthenware pots are gathered for a group portrait. The porcelain is glazed with ash, celadon, and cobalt, and the earthenware has a variety of finishing details; it's precisely these differences that make the pots look so lovely together.

FRESH PASTA

I enjoyed the feel of dough in my hands long before I learned to make ceramics. When I am moving back and forth between the studio and the house, I have to make sure to thoroughly wash my hands so that the clay does not get into what I am kneading in the kitchen! I bought an Atlas pasta machine when I was twenty years old, and it has been with me, still in its original box, in every house I've lived in since. It is one of those beautifully designed utilitarian objects that do not age. When I want to serve something special, I pull it out of the cabinet.

Fresh pasta is a delicious treat that can be prepared ahead of time and taken out of the freezer at the last moment to cook. I like to serve it with a simple roasted tomato sauce (page 151) and freshly grated Parmesan so the flavor comes through as clear as can be. *Makes enough for 2 for dinner, or 4 for a light lunch*

1 cup (125 g) all-purpose flour, plus more for
    kneading and rolling
1 large organic egg, plus 2 or 3 egg yolks
Fine cornmeal, for dusting
Pasta sauce, for serving
Salt, for the cooking water

SPECIAL EQUIPMENT
Pasta machine
Cutting attachment (optional)

Place the flour in a large bowl and make a well in the center. Crack the whole egg into the well, then add 2 egg yolks. Using a fork, swirl the flour into the eggs to form a damp mass.

With your fingers, gather the dough into a ball in the bowl. If some flour has not been incorporated and the dough is stiff and dry, add a third yolk and draw in the rest of the flour. It is okay if the ball is a bit sticky; it's better for it to be too wet than too dry at the start.

Dust a wooden board with flour and drop the ball onto the board. Knead by hand for about 5 minutes, drawing in the flour on the board, if necessary, until the stickiness disappears. The dough should be smooth and soft. Wrap the dough in a piece of plastic wrap, and let it sit for at least 45 minutes.

Lay a long sheet of parchment paper across your work surface and clamp the pasta machine to the side.

continued

Pull off a golf ball–size piece of dough from the ball and dust it with flour. (Working a smaller amount through the machine is much easier than starting with a big clump.) Keep the main dough ball covered, to prevent it from drying out.

Set the machine opening to 1 (the widest setting). Flatten the ball of dough into a pancake and run it through a few times. If the dough still seems damp or sticky, dust it with flour. Then change the opening to 2 and run the dough through again.

Continue making the opening smaller by changing to 3 and then 4; when you reach 5, run the dough through twice. Keep dusting with flour, if necessary. If for some reason the dough catches in the rollers, pull it out, dust it with flour, and start again back at the 1 setting, being sure to use your fingers to clean the dough stuck on the rollers so that it does not catch on the next round.

By this time, the dough should be long and thin. Using a kitchen knife, cut this sheet into two parts lengthwise so that it's more manageable (note that this will shorten the length of your pasta strands). Dust with flour again and run each part through the opening set at 6.

Put the two sheets of pasta through the cutting attachment, if using, or take the knife and hand-cut the thin dough into strips.

Dust the cut pasta with a bit of cornmeal to keep the strands separate. If the weather is damp and humid, immediately put the pasta on a tray and place in the freezer. (Add to the tray as each ball is processed through the machine.) The dough is fragile, and this keeps everything fresh.

Pull off another piece of dough from the ball. Open the pasta machine back to setting 1, the widest opening, and start again. Continue until all the dough has gone through the machine. Place all the finished cut pasta in the freezer until ready to use. (I often prepare the pasta a few days ahead of the meal.)

To cook and serve the pasta, warm your preferred pasta sauce in a large skillet. Fill a large stockpot (with an inset strainer, if you have one) with water and bring to a boil. When the water boils, stir in a few tablespoons of salt, remove the pasta from the freezer, and place it directly into the boiling water. Once the water boils again, the pasta will take only a minute or two to cook. Pull out a strand and taste. Drain the pasta, then gently place it in the skillet with the sauce and swirl to coat.

Seeking the Soul of Porcelain

After experimenting with high-fire translucent porcelain for more than a decade, I decided it was important to visit Jingdezhen, China, where porcelain originated and has been produced for millennia. Contemporary potters continue to follow the original production methods. I wanted to comprehend firsthand the origins and development of this elegant clay body.

I received a one-month residency at the Pottery Workshop, an international program that welcomes foreign artists to work with the artisans of Jingdezhen. There I observed the entire manufacturing process, from the mining of porcelain in the mountains surrounding the city to its firing in massive communal kilns. The small factories that produced the molds and made the pots were within walking distance of the residency compound. At the Jingdezhen kiln museum, I saw reconstructed examples of ovens, from ancient wood-fired kilns known as anagamas up to present-day models, and learned how the potters fired the porcelain in such large quantities.

On that trip, I began to think of the Chinese pottery tradition as a kind of conceptual art form. The production process represents a vast collaboration rather than a collection of unique work by individual potters. Each step relies on an artisan who completes just that particular aspect of the whole. First one person creates the pot design and hands off the drawing to the fabricators. Then there is a thrower, a mold maker, a trimmer, a caster, a decorator, a glazer, and a person who maintains the kilns. All pots are glazed while still raw (they are not put through the bisque stage) and fired in the communal kilns. No piece is signed: Everyone's pots are placed together, and each one emerges anonymously to join thousands of others like it. The majority of visiting artists at the residency embraced this manufacturing approach and worked with the artisans to produce ceramics for exhibitions. Some of them return every year with new designs.

I think of my time in Jingdezhen and reference many things I learned. The production strategy did not appeal to me in terms of my own process, however, because I continually assess and adjust a pot as it moves through each step. I'm not willing to concede this decision making, because it's integral to the finished piece.

I was happy to have experienced this communal porcelain culture nevertheless. In starting any creative endeavor, it's important to know your own nature. The exploration reaffirmed my sense of my own path, but I also learned some valuable techniques (such as painting with cobalt and how to trim porcelain when it is virtually dry).

During my residency in Jingdezhen, I learned about the history of cobalt painting from a young painting master named Huang Fei. I made these porcelain pieces at his studio, using his variety of cobalt stains, before they were fired in the communal kiln.

The Allure of Glazes

Through lots of trial and a fair amount of error, I have managed to teach myself the necessary techniques to produce my particular ceramics. And though I am not adept at developing mathematical formulas, I am an avid detective when it comes to discovering glaze recipes to try. I love to collect glaze books and manuals and study the possibilities within. If I had my way, I would concoct glazes all day long.

There is an enormous archive of glazes in the world, both historic and contemporary. I particularly admire the work of two twentieth-century masters, Brother Thomas Bezanson and Shōji Hamada. Brother Thomas, an exceptional technician, took classic Chinese formulas, including oxblood and celadon, and transformed them into something specifically modern by applying them to large, sophisticated, sleek forms. But Brother Thomas kept his glaze notebooks a secret, so I'm left to search for possible formulas to unlock the mystery of the luminous quality his pots possess. Japanese potter Shōji Hamada also worked with classic Chinese as well as Japanese recipes. His work, unlike Brother Thomas's, is somewhat rough, a result of his aesthetic and use of wood-kiln firing.

Clay bodies and glazes that can be fired to 2345°F (1285°C) interest me most because I like to work with porcelain that vitrifies. At this temperature, the clay loses all porosity, and the glazes that can be used are elegant and translucent. This temperature is known as cone 10, which refers to the pyrometric cone placed inside the kiln. At 2345°F (1285°C), a cone marked 10 will bend over, which lets the potter know that the correct temperature has been reached. (Made up of composite materials, pyrometric cones are designed to gauge the kiln atmosphere starting at 1087°F/586°C and going all the way to 2464°F/1351°C.)

My Geil gas kiln fires in a reduction atmosphere. This means that through the use of a damper and gas, I control the amount of oxygen in the kiln. As the oxygen is burned off, the flame seeks the oxygen molecules in the glaze and clay body to keep going. This atmosphere is necessary to create the types of glazes I find most appealing.

Whichever glaze I use, my first rule of thumb is to avoid toxic chemicals. Even so, I still wear a mask when measuring out ingredients to avoid inhaling particles, and store all the necessary supplies in large, well-marked buckets in the glaze-making area of my studio.

It can take my clients a while to move with me into new glazes. I was hand-painting my pieces with flowers and fruit when I began my business; when I started emphasizing the white clay and forms without my drawings, everyone balked. Now those unadorned pieces are some

Slight variations in the chemicals or ash content of a glaze can create a range of color and texture. I used this group of small tiles to test different ash glaze recipes, in search of a pale blue with a crackled surface.

of the most popular. I want to work with new recipes for glazes such as oxblood, but I'm pulled between experimentation and what clients want. I suppose that's business. But I trust that slowly but surely, people will begin to respond to these pieces as well.

Following are the most tried-and-true (and beautiful) glazes I work with.

ORIBE

The first oribe pottery was made during the Keichō era (1596–1615) in Japan and is said to be named after the general and tea master Furuta Oribe. The glaze has a deep green hue, created by the high-fired copper in the recipe. Oribe presents itself differently depending on the clay body and whether it is fired in a gas or wood kiln but always retains a beautiful green color. I often pair the glaze with oxblood and ash, as shown on page 73, as these combinations create wonderful contrasts and vibrancy.

OXBLOOD

This bloodred glaze is elusive to achieve. Oxblood was first developed in China during the Ming dynasty (1368–1644). It disappeared for a time and then came back into use during the Qing Dynasty (1644–1922). At the end of the nineteenth century, French art nouveau potters made masterpieces with their version of this glaze, called *sang de boeuf.* Copper in the glaze causes

These bud vases illustrate the rich oranges and blacks in the shino glaze. How each pot will respond to the reduced-carbon kiln atmosphere is unknown, and only revealed once the kiln is unpacked. This particular recipe is a classic known as Malcolm's Shino.

it to turn red during the firing; the glaze is fugitive, however, meaning the pot has to be in just the right position in the kiln for the rich red color to appear. I usually surround oxblood pots with other oxblood or celadon pots; this cocooning seems to make them happy. The color that results has many shades of red, purple, green, and blue within it. I use three or four different recipes for oxblood, and the finished pots look gorgeous arranged together.

CELADON

This iconic glaze usually contains iron oxide for coloring, yet depending upon the percentage and other possible colorants, a vast variation of shades—from pale green to deep blue—can result. Celadon glazes were first produced during the Northern Song dynasty (960–1127), but the glaze and hue changed during subsequent dynasties, depending on where in China the kilns were located. Celadon made its way to Japan, Korea, and eventually Europe. I have some wonderful celadon recipes and intend to keep experimenting until I achieve the brightest and most translucent blue, a shade known as "sky after rain" in China.

SHINO

This glaze emerged around the sixteenth century in the Mino province of Japan. It is a thick, white-orange matte glaze with wonderful variation that depends, like other glazes, on the kiln atmosphere and the position of pot and shelves. To bring out its deep orange and black colors, shino glaze appreciates a reduction atmosphere where the oxygen is largely deprived and carbon smoke is produced. I am a great admirer of the late American potter Warren MacKenzie's shino recipes.

ASH GLAZES

A significant portion of any ash glaze recipe must be composed of burnt organic material such as plant leaves or wood. The chemical composition of the material affects the color and body of the glaze. I am fascinated by ash glazes and have been playing with them for the last year or two, inspired by the work of Katherine Pleydell-Bouverie. In the 1930s, Pleydell-Bouverie concocted ash glazes from trees and shrubs on her farm in England and applied them to her beautiful pots. She left a great list of the plants on her farm, and I have been slowly trying to use similar ones, burning all sorts of trees and flowers. Friends kindly bring their apple, quince, and pear tree branches for these glaze experiments. My favorite aspect of ash-glazed pots is the beautiful crackle that results from the firing, which is caused by the different contractions of the glaze to the clay as the pot cools down. The ash from the trees on our property produces a beautiful pale blue crackle.

The gorgeous red of the oxblood glaze shimmers on these porcelain vases. When examined at close range, each one displays a complex array of colors that contributes to its vibrancy.

Celadon produces serene colors, with subtle changes in the glaze formula resulting in hues ranging from green to blue and even yellow. Variations are due in part to the red or yellow iron oxide percentage in the recipe, which creates the intensity of hue.

Oribe is a true chameleon, its color varying enormously depending on the clay. It appears as a brilliant green blue when fired over white porcelain (see the vase on the far left and the bowl in front; both were also brushed with oxblood, for contrast). Stoneware absorbs the light, bringing out a deep forest green in the glaze (as on the pot in the center front; its top was brushed with ash glaze).

The depth of the blue in this assembly of ash vases depends on the thickness of the glaze and the location of the kiln flame. I dipped the necks of some into oxblood to add a bit of contrast.

Throwing a Pot, Step-by-Step

When I conceive of a pot, it usually lends itself to being produced on the wheel. Throwing is my starting point and the technique with which I am most comfortable, though I do hand build as well (see page 90). Here, I demonstrate the process of creating one of my most popular pots. I sometimes name a pot after the person or place associated with its creation, as it helps me identify it easily. This shape was first designed at the request of a friend, Sabine Rothman; she asked for a bit of a pedestal and some beads, and thus, the Sabine was born. Its slightly oval shape is wonderful for flowers.

1. Measure out the amount of clay for the main body of the pot, then wedge (knead) it on a board to remove air pockets and encourage plasticity for throwing.

2. Place the wedged clay on the wheel and center it.

3. After the clay is centered, bring up the sides of the clay. It usually takes two or three pulls to get the desired height for the body.

4. Once the height of the pot is achieved, use a rubber rib to smooth off the clay sides.

5. Just after throwing the body of the vase, make the pedestal (so that the two parts dry at the same time).

6. Move the pedestal off the bat so that the bottom dries evenly.

7. Trim both the body and the pedestal as soon as they can be handled without collapsing.

8. Join the pieces together with slip (clay that is of a cream consistency) and clay.

9. Push the vase's body into an oval shape. This must be done while the clay is fairly soft so that the rim does not crack.

10. Form each handle by rolling a small piece of clay into a log, then closing the ends together into a circle. Attach the handles to each side with a bit of slip, and smooth them firmly against the main body.

11. With a small bit of clay, roll beads and place them along the rim.

12. Watch the vase carefully as it dries so that it remains straight.

Eight Finishing Touches

Throwing is just the beginning of creating a pot. Once the piece is trimmed and ready for detailing, the exciting part begins. It might sound corny, but I feel that every pot tells me what I need to do to finish it. As a result, each one is distinct. It is the essence of my collaboration with the clay, the back-and-forth in the creative process. What follows are a few of the elements that I consistently add to my work, and that define my ceramic vocabulary.

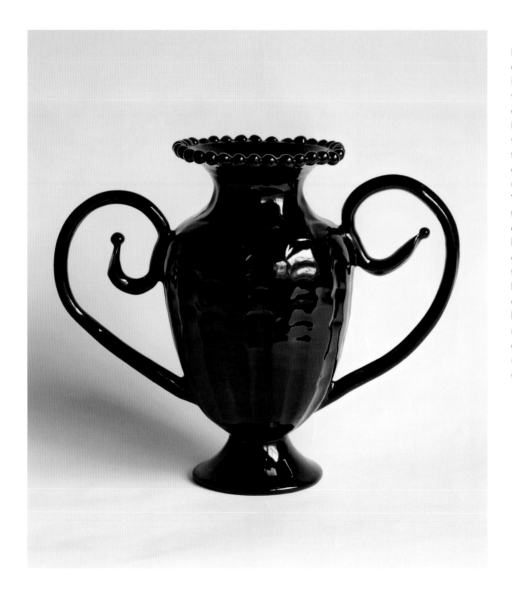

1. HANDLES

Handles can be functional or decorative—or both. In every instance, a handle must work with the design of the body of the pot it is connected to. If it will need to support the weight of a mug or a pitcher, the handle must be sturdy and attached firmly to the body, usually with an extra bit of clay. The thickness of the handles on the white pitchers opposite, for example, is proportional to the heft of the forms. When creating embellished handles, I often twirl the clay into rounds or loops, to lend whimsy to the pot's overall character. The handles on the black vase at left, inspired by the masterful handles of Cycladic and Etruscan potters, can be used to pick up the vase, but they are also fantastical.

2. PEDESTALS

Pedestals are quite important in my work. The first examples I studied were on early Wedgwood vessels and the impressive marble urns at the Vatican in Rome. The height and width of a pedestal in relation to the form of the vase or bowl can make all the difference in the visual impact. I like pedestals to be as dramatic as possible, though first and foremost, the pedestal's primary purpose—to support the pot—must be considered. The hand-built square pedestal opposite is a strong contrast to the thrown porcelain vase that sits on top. The pedestal on the piece below is a more neoclassic design, to complement the wide fluted bowl.

3. BEADING

I first started putting beads around the edge of my earthenware pots to protect the rims from chips, to which the low-fire clay is susceptible. Over time, the beading became a signature detail of my work. I have rolled thousands and thousands of beads, one at a time. Though I personally gravitate toward pots with a simpler design, beadwork is the finish most requested by clients, and I am happy to comply. Most of the time, I place the beads all the way around a vase, bowl, or platter, but opposite are a few variations on this decorative touch. I especially enjoy making sawtooth cutouts topped with beads, which are evocative of one of my favorite photographs, a 1957 "milk splash" by Harold Edgerton.

4. HOLES

Holes create a lightness in the overall feeling of a vessel. I use tubing in various diameters (see page 115) to cut into the clay when it is leather-hard. Usually, I place the holes at the edge of a pot so that they do not disrupt its utility. When I make a bowl to hold fruit or vegetables, I will poke holes throughout the body, to allow air to circulate.

5. RUFFLES

Years ago, I went to an exhibition in Venice of artist Anselm Kiefer's large-scale lead book sculptures. I was captivated by their edges, which created a rippling and pliable effect. Hoping to produce a similar effect with clay, I rolled it out in wide, thin strips, then folded and placed them on the edges of a pot. My clients started calling these trimmings ruffles, a name that has stuck.

6. FLUTING

I am particularly attached to two loop tools (see page 115) that I use to create fluting designs on the pots. The lines are always irregular, as I do not lay out my pattern but instead dive into the carving spontaneously. When the pots are thrown, the walls must be fairly thick so that the gouging does not put a hole in the side. One simple tool can create a variety of effects, as seen in the group of pots opposite.

7. SCULPTURAL GESTURES

Like one of my ceramics heroes, George Ohr, I aspire to throw paper-thin pots with a good deal of textural expression. The best time to alter a vessel is right after its walls have been pulled up, while the clay is at its most elastic and malleable. I put one hand inside the pot and the other directly outside, and then push and pinch the clay to make an undulating surface. If I am working in porcelain, the thinness of the stretched clay makes it more translucent, and when the finished pot is held up to light, one can see a transparency where my fingers have been. The grouping of porcelain vases above illustrates how the lines formed by my fingers create shadows on the surfaces of the celadon pots.

8. DRAWING AND PAINTING

The ceramics made by the Omega Workshops in England were my incentive to learn pottery. My earliest pieces were painted with underglazes on white earthenware clay, which acted as a blank canvas. In this pot, which I made in 1997, I used the clay like a sketch pad for black charcoal lines. More recently, I received a commission to design a collection referencing the decoration on Cycladic pottery (opposite), and it was refreshing to embellish the earthenware once more—this time with low-fire underglaze.

Building a Pot, Step-by-Step

Although the majority of my work is thrown on the wheel, some shapes demand to be hand built. I enjoy thinking up odd designs to construct from patterns or molds. Usually, the finished piece involves a combination of elements thrown on the wheel and constructed parts that are then joined together. These hand-built pots typically end up being a bit asymmetrical, which lends them a welcome sense of humor. Here's how a trapezoidal vase is built.

1. Make a trapezoidal form to your desired dimensions out of a firm cardboard. Then roll out a sufficient amount of clay on a board to accommodate the template four times. Using a needle tool, trace the template to cut out each of the four sides of the vase.

2. Using clay and slip (clay that is of a cream consistency), join the four sides.

3. After the four sides are assembled, roll strips of clay and place them on the inside of the panels to further hold them together. You need enough clay to fit in the crevice of the entire length of each side to secure each side to the next.

4. Turn the piece upside down and apply pressure on the outside to make it as symmetrical as possible.

5. Apply a roll of clay over each seam, on the outside, to hold the panels together.

6. Roll out a small amount of clay on a board and place the trapezoid form on top. Using the needle tool, cut out a square of clay slightly larger than the bottom of the vase and attach it to the main body with slip and additional rolls of clay. Smooth up the excess clay around the bottom of the trapezoid and smooth with the rib.

7. Using a loop tool, carve fluted lines into the sides of the trapezoid.

8. Separately throw the pedestal. When both the vase and the pedestal are leather hard (depending on the air conditions in the studio, which vary enormously), put them together with slip and again a roll of clay. Once the vase has dried thoroughly, it is ready to be fired.

Hand building works well with shapes and sizes of all sorts. The pair of white earthenware square vases at left was inspired by classic Chinese brush pots. I ribbed the sides with the loop tool (see page 115). The unusually shaped terra-cotta piece opposite pays homage to one of my favorites from the Greek galleries in the Metropolitan Museum. It works perfectly with forced bulbs like amaryllis, which do not need to be covered in soil to sprout flowers.

The Value of My Work

Pricing my work has been a challenge from the beginning. It is hard to say "I am worth this!" There is a dance between what I want to be paid for a pot and what the market will bear. It has taken decades to craft a strategy that feels true to my efforts.

At the outset of my business, my dear late friend Linda Lee Johnson, a jewelry designer, advised that after determining the material and labor costs associated with a piece, you should arrive at a price that will allow you to feel fairly compensated for your efforts. This is an ongoing consideration—never a rote exercise.

As a general rule, I do not reduce the price of my work, put it on sale, or sell "seconds." And I would rather not barter, preferring to pay someone for their services, as I wish to be paid in return.

As mindful as I am about valuing my work, I am respectful of the fact that customers have entrusted me with their funds to receive a pot in exchange. I answer correspondence about orders as quickly as possible and update customers if their pots are taking longer than usual to produce or to ship. On the (thankfully) rare instance when a client wishes to return or exchange a pot, I refund their money or happily offer to make something new.

I often think of the line "It's not personal, it's business" in *You've Got Mail*. Tom Hanks's character's mega-bookstore has just put Meg Ryan's character's small bookshop out of business, and he (channeling *The Godfather*) assures her that it was nothing personal. But it *was* personal to her, as my business has always been to me. It defines my integrity as an artist. Every pot sent out into the world is an extension of myself. I take orders seriously, and I take pride in the knowledge that I have done my very best. I believe that this energy flows through the clay and is present in all that I create. And I hope that this is what my customers respond to when they receive their vessels.

The stairs from the ground floor of my studio, where I produce my pots, to the second floor, where I display and ship finished work, is a way station of sorts. I often place completed pieces on the bottom steps, to be brought upstairs a few at a time. The same goes for books, journals, or gardening tools.

The Meditation of Repetition

Since childhood, I've watched the same movies and read the same books many times over. With each viewing or reading, I discover a different idea or inspiration. My understanding of the artist or author deepens, and I appreciate the work all the more. It is a similar exploration with my pottery—through my repetition of forms,

I find an aspect in the making that I had not previously imagined. And there are recipes I've made so many times I could prepare them blindfolded, yet they never taste exactly the same.

I have thrown thousands of pots over the years, including some shapes I form again and again. I work in the studio

practically every day, yet I never find it boring or monotonous—in fact, I look forward to showing up each morning.

I once attended a lecture by the artist Carrie Mae Weems, and she clarified something I had long been trying to define. In discussing how artists explore the same theme over and over, she mentioned that Louis Armstrong recorded "Saint Louis Blues" more than eighty times, each version with a different sound. This helped me understand why each time I'm making a pot—no matter how large or small or how often I've made the same shape—I learn something new and find a fresh way to articulate my intention.

The Shane pot shown here was inspired by an eighth-century Chinese design. I was captivated by its simplicity and modernity, its proportions, and the expressiveness of its handles.

TARTE TATIN

In the summer of 2001, I was determined to learn how to make a tarte tatin, that heavenly dessert of caramelized fruit and pastry. I researched numerous recipes and approaches, including Julia Child's, but did not succeed in finding one that tasted best and had the easiest technique. I made a tarte tatin every day for a month, testing and not quite achieving the right balance. Then I came across a simple recipe that had run in the *New York Times* in November 2000. I have been making a variation of it ever since, using my mother's dough recipe. (You can substitute store-bought puff pastry, if you wish.) I prefer to use a light-colored skillet, as it is easier to see the sugar changing color than in a cast-iron pan. The original recipe called for six apples, but I find that seven or eight (if small) better fill the skillet and the tart looks prettier once inverted. *Makes one 10-inch (25 cm) tart; serves 8 to 10*

All-purpose flour, for dusting
Pie dough from the Goat Cheese and Leek
    Tart (see page 30), chilled
3 tablespoons (42 g) unsalted butter,
    at room temperature

⅓ cup (133 g) sugar
7 or 8 medium Gala or Golden Delicious
    apples, peeled, cored, and quartered
Ice cream or whipped cream, for serving
    (optional)

Preheat the oven to 375°F (190°C).

Lightly flour a work surface, then roll the chilled dough into a 12-inch (30 cm) round about ⅛ inch (3 mm) thick. With an offset spatula, spread the butter evenly over the bottom of a 10-inch (25 cm) heavy ovenproof skillet (or a tarte tatin mold, if you have one). Sprinkle with the sugar, turning the pan to coat it evenly.

Beginning from the outer edge of the pan, arrange the apples, peeled sides down, in concentric circles, fitting them closely together. Place the pan over low heat until the butter melts, then increase the heat to medium-high and cook, without stirring, until the sugar turns a rich brown color. (The *Times* recipe says 30 minutes, but I watch the color of the sugar and wait for the burnt-sugar smell. You can push the cooking time a bit further than you think; trial and error will teach you how to judge.) Remove the skillet from the heat and press gently on the apples with a wooden spoon to close up any spaces between them.

Place the dough over the apples, tucking around the edge to fit it just inside the pan. Bake for 20 to 25 minutes, until the pastry is golden brown. To unmold, run a thin knife around the inside edge of the pan. Place a serving platter over the pan, then immediately invert it to release the tart. If any apples have stuck to the pan, gently remove them and reposition them on the tart. Serve warm, topped with ice cream or whipped cream, if you wish.

ON LAUGHTER

About fifteen years ago, while visiting family in Florida for Christmas, my daughter and I took a class in qigong with a local instructor. This centuries-old practice uses movement, breathing, and rhythmic postures to improve one's mental health and well-being. The teacher told us that it is important to have a big, full belly laugh each day. He had a deep, infectious bass "ha-ha-ha," and he made us all produce the same while in the class. It did seem to release a good spirit into the air. Ever since, I try to find something joyful or funny every day that makes me laugh out loud.

The physical act of the strong guffaw does wonders to refresh the body and send oxygen surging through it again. I have also come to realize that a key component to the laugh of the day is sharing it with someone. When I find myself straying into a bit of a funk (usually due to tiredness), I meet or call a friend. The companionship and humor go well beyond the laugh to restore my sense of calm. I am reminded that all is not bleak, and there is always a ray of light to be found. Even the smallest funny thing can bring long-lasting delight.

I also hope my pots contain a bit of lightness and humor that emanate when they are part of a home. The combination of fanciful flowers and whimsical vase always produces a smile!

PART II

ROUTINE IS EVERYTHING

Consistency is essential to my creative life and I am out in the studio every day. Or rather, I am drawn there without conscious effort—I long to be there, always.

Sometimes in the midst of my work, I have to stop and walk outside. Although ostensibly I plant flowers to give context to the pots in my photographs, I grow them as much for my peace of mind. The ability to go stand in the garden, to just be there in the quiet and think, is fundamental to my approach to making. It is the balance to the constant effort to produce. Last summer, in the early mornings, I marveled at a hummingbird that regularly visited my gardens. I heard it coming as I stood among the tennis court beds, its wings beating impossibly fast, and watched as it kissed each blossom that it chose to alight upon. That moment of intense beauty gave me the sense of tranquility to head back into the studio, ready to begin again.

Working from Home

When I first began making pots, my wheel was in the middle of the children's playroom, and they were moving around me most of the time. My tiny electric kiln was just outside on the deck, in all weather. Pots were perched everywhere. It was clear that I needed to come up with a different strategy to organize and separate my new passion from our living space. At the same time, our family had outgrown the house itself. With three children and a large dog, Wally and I decided to look for a place that would better suit our needs. He found an 1850s colonial house on the opposite side of town that had plenty of room for everyone, as well as sunny, flat land for a garden.

My first proper studio was set up in the basement of that old colonial, and it was much more conducive to working. The house's stone foundation comprised my studio walls. Windows facing the back of the property allowed the sun to stream in during the day. One might think that the room was part of a Provençal home based on the photos taken at this period. The excellent location also allowed me to hear the children upstairs and to be available quickly whenever they needed me. I worked well there for ten years.

Next to the house was a garage that had been used as a horse barn by the previous owners. It was in terrible shape. After living with the eyesore for a decade, Wally proposed taking it down and building a work barn in its place.

He found a builder who specialized in restoring old house frames. The man located a 1790s house in a nearby town and moved the beams to our property. A large crane lifted them into place, then the floors and walls were added. The barn took almost a year to construct.

The original plan was for me to use the first floor as my studio and for the upstairs to be a family room. By the time the barn was finished, however, the children were teenagers and had no interest in hanging out anywhere near us. So little by little, my finished pots migrated upstairs. I used the open space to pack pots for shipping, and in no time at all, I had completely overtaken the barn, much to Wally's chagrin. But he has been incredibly supportive about it all, truth be told.

Although the barn is just a stone's throw from the house, it feels as if it's a world away, a separate space I'm able to step into and focus. Once inside, I am fully present in the studio and can take on the tasks that need to be completed. Its proximity to the house also allows me to tend to projects outside of regular work hours, if needed, without having to leave home. The same is true of the garden; when I enter the beds, I am able to mentally differentiate them from both the home and work environments, though they all exist within a relatively small radius.

The wheel dedicated to earthenware clay and the table I use for photography are in close proximity. I like to study pots in front of me as I throw and watch the light change outside, waiting for the optimal shooting moment. It is a good example of the interplay between my ceramics and the photos, with the flowers from the garden a key link between the two.

Everything in
Its Place

It has taken more than thirty years to
develop a studio that suits my work
process. Ultimately, I consider it an
investment to design a well-functioning
workspace. The adage "It takes money
to make money" remains my motto
regarding new equipment, all of which
I acquire and pay for with my pottery
earnings.

   Once I moved into the barn studio,
I purchased two wheels to supplement
my first so that each clay type (white
earthenware, terra-cotta, and porcelain)
had its own machine. I am not a neat
thrower; having multiples alleviates the
need to clean whenever I change clay
bodies, which saves time. The wheels are
placed along the east-facing wall, with
large windows that are cranked open in
warm weather. I can follow the arc of the
sun across the day. The whole space is
peaceful and quiet, except for the sound
of the birds outside.

   I already owned two electric kilns
that were used at our first house; these
are placed together on the other side
of the room, away from the wheels.
Because the property's overall electrical
system was upgraded when the barn was
constructed, I now have enough wattage
to fire both electric kilns simultaneously,

if necessary. In busy periods, like just before my annual open studio or the holiday season, the kilns run nonstop.

The construction crew made an outbuilding behind the barn to hold a gas kiln. A second propane tank was required for the kiln and barn, separate from the house. And, deciding it was time to embark on a new challenging adventure, I recently built a wood-fired kiln (see page 236) and am now learning and experimenting with how the ash and wood flame affect the surface of pots and glazes.

A dedicated building, wheel, and kilns are not necessarily available to everyone, of course. The important thing is to find what works for you, and to proceed incrementally as you gain knowledge and experience. Getting your hands in the clay is what matters. The following essentials should help you get started.

- A room with light and good air circulation; if you wish to make your own glazes, you'll need a designated area for chemicals, plus dual cartridge respirators for mixing.

- A pottery wheel and its supportive equipment, if you wish to throw, or a worktable if you plan to be a hand builder.

- A safe, uncluttered spot to leave the work as it dries.

- Ideally, a kiln of some sort, whether used or new. For potters just starting out, a communal kiln might be the best bet. It's also a great way to share information with others about making and firing pots.

This beautiful update of a Shaker woodstove, made by Wittus, provides not only warmth but also a great place to think. I can step away from the wheel, stand by the heat, and contemplate my next move. When the weather is cold and damp, the stove also serves to dry the pots (though it's safer to place them in front of, rather than on top of, the stove).

Day In, Day Out

I wake up most mornings at five o'clock, even in the dark of winter. I will be out in the garden before sunrise during the summer months, sometimes by four thirty. I love picking flowers—shortly to be used in photographs taken in the studio—just as the sun comes over the trees.

I've always been an early riser. I like to think that I take after my grandmother, who grew up on a dairy. She delivered milk with a horse and wagon before school every morning. Afterward, she would ride to school, then she'd pat the horse on the back and it would make its way home while she went to class. I, too, was probably a farmer in another life. My internal clock works well with an "early to bed, early to rise" routine. My father was also a morning person. We would have coffee (I was given coffee with lots of milk as a girl; my habit stems from about age five) and read the *New York Times* together in silence every day.

Morning remains my favorite time of day. I do my best thinking from five to seven a.m. I have coffee with Wally while I make a list of things to be done. After those early-morning photo sessions, my next task is whatever *must* happen that day, whether it is glazing and firing a load of pots or answering mail. I prioritize the obligation that requires the most attention or is the least pleasant to fulfill. The goal is to get the hard stuff out of the way while my energy is fresh and I am least apt to cut corners or make mistakes.

I try to go to a barre class in town or do some other type of exercise three or four mornings a week. The class provides needed socialization, because I will be in the studio alone the rest of the day. I've become friends with the women in the class, and we discuss our current woes and small victories. The exercise keeps me mentally and physically fit, which is important, because working in the studio requires the strength to move clay, glaze buckets, and packed boxes, and the stamina to get through long to-do lists.

If I don't go anywhere first, I enter the studio at five thirty or six a.m. I am always excited to start working, and time flies by. If there is no pressing obligation, I like to throw first thing (because throwing takes the most concentration). Or I trim and put together pots that have pedestals so that I can watch them closely as they dry throughout the day, to keep them straight. (There is a moment when the clay is too dry to shift, but up until that point, I can correct a piece to keep it erect. If I combine a pot's parts too late in the day, they will dry overnight, when I can't monitor their movement.) I throw plates at this time, as well; the rims pull up as they dry and have to be put back on the wheel to move the rims down again.

I break for lunch at midday and put something simple together. When I was in elementary school, I would walk home for lunch every day and eat a shredded iceberg lettuce salad. This is my Proustian madeleine moment, so I usually have a chopped salad to honor that childhood memory.

After lunch, I return to the studio—though I must confess that if the schedule permits, I take a nap first. I can close my eyes for fifteen or twenty minutes and awaken without an alarm, completely refreshed. Since I get up so early, this nap helps me power through what is a very long day.

I try to do my shipping right after lunch, while I still have sufficient energy and there's enough sunlight left to see well (especially important during the short days of winter). Packing the pots is a critical part of production. In the past, I hired people to help me, but when things began arriving to clients broken, I decided to incorporate this part of the process into my schedule. There's no point in spending a vast amount of time making work only to have it damaged in transit. I actually enjoy the mathematical process of packing. Since every pot is a different size, the pot-to-box ratio has to be calculated for each order. Years ago, the Takashimaya design store returned some work to me; they had wrapped each piece in bubble wrap and then newsprint before placing it in the box.

I've since adapted this packing method, using an added layer of corrugated cardboard instead of an interior box. This allows for sufficient protection plus the flexibility to accommodate the individual shapes of the pieces.

By three o'clock, I am ready for a cup of tea. I need a bit of caffeine to keep me going. At this point, I am either glazing pieces to be fired or sitting back down at the wheel. (If I throw a simple design at the end of the day, I can leave it uncovered and it will be at the perfect stage for trimming when I return the next morning.) I keep going at one thing or another. During the spring, summer, or fall months, I head outside late in the afternoon to care for the flowers. It is not as hot then and really pleasant to be in the garden.

I try to finish up in the studio by six or six thirty in the evening. In the warmer months, I often take photographs at this time (in addition to the morning ones) because the light is perfect. Otherwise, I head into the house, looking forward to a glass of wine. I love an uneventful evening that allows for an early bedtime. Wally or I make dinner, then I read or watch a movie before heading off to sleep, eager to greet the day ahead.

Essential Equipment

Although my hands are the tools I rely on the most, I learned to throw with a small group of pottery tools, which remain in my basic arsenal. Below and on the following pages are other objects that serve as extensions of my hands. Together, they help me accomplish all the necessary tasks in the studio.

MAKING TOOLS

1. Rolling pin. I use rolling pins when making hand-formed slab pots and platters. I keep separate pins for earthenware, porcelain, and terra-cotta.

2. Synthetic sponge. My favorite, most indispensable implement is this sponge, which costs about a dollar. I use it at every phase of production—from throwing to smoothing to propping up handles and cake plates as they dry.

3. Needle tool. When throwing, I use the needle tool to even off the top edge of a newly thrown shape if it is a little wonky, and to mark the width of a foot.

4 and 13. Rubber ribs. Mudtools produces the most wonderful rubber ribs for throwing both the inside and outside of a pot. I use the stiff blue rib most often, to even off the outside of a pot and create a straight edge. The softer red rib tool is lovely for smoothing off clay where two parts are joined.

5. Handmade plastic tool. The rarest of all my tools, this was made by the husband of a friend from New Zealand. I use it to reach inside a freshly thrown pot to pull out ribs.

6 and 9. Throwing sticks. These wooden sticks, with curved hooks or knobs at the ends, are used to round out the belly of a pot after its neck has been narrowed. They are pushed in, tilted, then dragged up the sides to make the piece wider.

7. Paintbrush. Paintbrushes can be used to remove excess water inside a pot or to smooth the outside after throwing.

8. Wooden cut-off stick. This tool removes excess clay at the bottom of the outside of a pot after throwing.

10. Wire tool. A wire tool is used to separate the pot from the wheel bat it was thrown upon.

11. Carving bow. This tool is used to create a facet (planed surface) shortly after the body is thrown. I leave the walls extra thick, then cut off the sides with the wire strung on the bow to give five to eight sides to what would otherwise be a round pot.

12. Tape measure. Since I usually throw a pot to specific dimensions, the tape measure is in constant use for checking width and height.

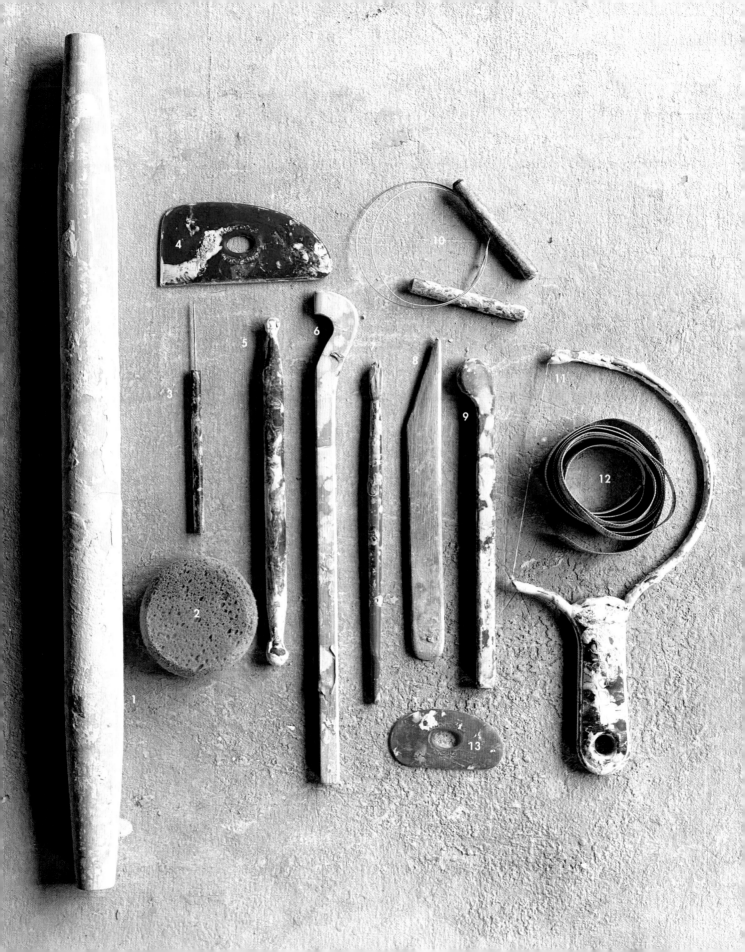

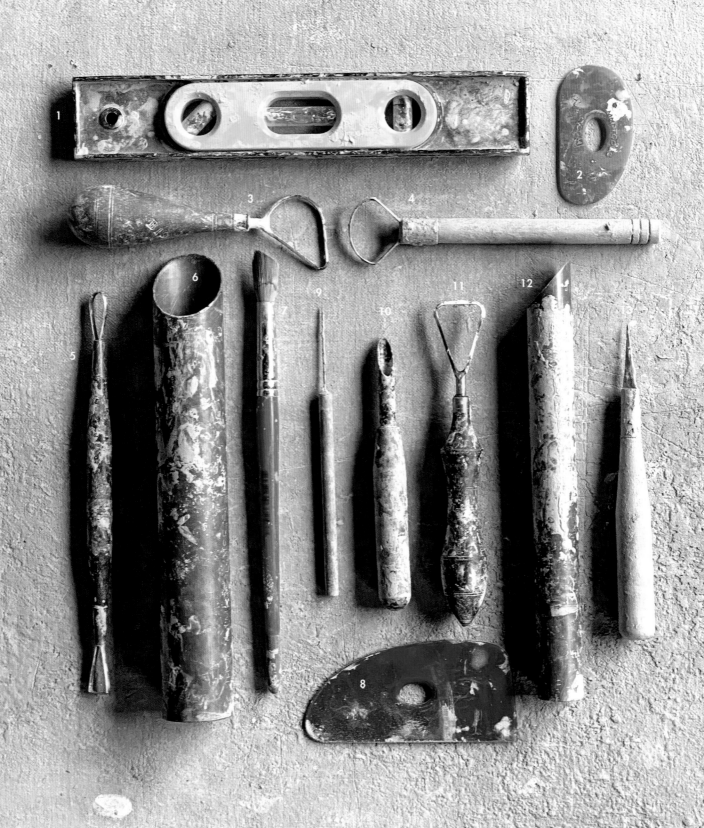

TRIMMING TOOLS

1. Small level. I use this on all pedestal pieces, to ensure that the plate or vase is level. This is not always apparent once the piece is finished, however, because clay shifts as it dries and fires. It's the nature of the process that the balance will never be perfect.

2 and 8. Rubber ribs. When assembling, I use these tools for smoothing down seams and areas where different joined parts are connected (see page 112 for more on ribs).

3 and 11. Bison trim tools. These beautiful trimmers were handmade by Philip Poburka's Bison Studios. I use the rounder one specifically for porcelain, as its sharpness allows for precise trimming on almost-dry porcelain pots. Because the carbon steel head is fragile, I store this tool carefully, so it won't fall and lose its tip. The triangular trim tool works very well for carving out the side of the foot and bottom of a pot.

4 and 5. Loop tools. The Dolan loop tool (4) is a great all-purpose shape. The Kemper 8R2 (5) is among my most-used tools; it's the perfect width for creating a foot out of a pot bottom.

6, 10, and 12. Hole cutters. I use these often, to cut round holes in my designs (see page 84 for an example of this effect). The copper cutters (6 and 12) were handmade from tubing by a friend a number of years ago.

7. Paintbrush. I rely on dozens of brushes in a vast range of types and sizes for different tasks at the trimming stage—glazing, applying slip to attach different parts to each other, and wetting an edge to attach clay balls.

9. Needle tool. When trimming, this tool is essential for slipping and scoring, a technique whereby you wet and then scratch lines into two clay parts that will be joined together.

13. Cut-out knife. I use this knife to carve jigsaw edges and cut round shapes, such as that of a pedestal, into a square form.

Handmade Molds

In addition to throwing on the wheel and hand building geometric pieces (see pages 76 and 90, respectively), I create clay molds to shape some of my pots. Once I have an idea for the structure, I build the model out of white earthenware (sometimes stuffing newsprint under it to help create the shape I'm after). If the finished piece will be round or oval (like the rightmost vases, opposite), I slice the mold in half. I then bisque-fire the mold or molds.

When it's time to create a pot, I drape raw clay over the mold. If I'm building the piece in two halves, once the clay is leather-hard I combine the two pieces with coils of clay and slip. Pedestals, necks, handles, or other details are thrown separately and joined at this stage, before the pot is left to dry. Though the forms are meant to be used repeatedly, no two molded pieces ever look quite the same.

My favorite molds (below) feature deep grooves and ribs and are inspired by springs, spirals, scallops, and even autumn squashes (the squat round one reminds me of a plump gourd). I am continually delighted by the transformation of the clay as it's shaped into dramatic, whimsical new vessels (opposite).

ON WORKING ROW BY ROW

When I was about eight years old, my mother taught me how to knit. I made simple scarves, then moved on to sweaters. In my twenties, I got orders from friends for knitted pieces, and since I was working full-time, I started to carry the knitting with me everywhere. At any opportunity, I'd knit a row or two, to advance the project. I thought of Gertrude Stein's phrase "a rose is a rose is a rose" but reframed it as "a row is a row is a row," meaning that if I had only a short period of time to work, just knitting one row at a time would eventually add up to the whole. This became my philosophy about life in general.

If I could have one magical thing from the Harry Potter books, it would be Hermione's Time-Turner, to allow the hours to repeat. The days go by too fast, and I wish I had more moments to spend in the studio, in the garden, in museums, reading books—you name it. If one considers the span of the day and the list of what needs to be accomplished, it is easier to break the items down into components. *A row is a row is a row* is a realistic way to approach tasks one by one. People have told me that they wished they could have done such and such, but they never had enough time. The truth is, there is *never* enough time, yet I find that these moments provide the best opportunity to maximize the minutes of the day.

I apply this mantra to cooking, gardening, and making ceramics. In the kitchen, for example, I will measure the ingredients for a cake or sprinkle salt and pepper over meat for a stew that I will put in the oven later. In the garden, if I can weed one area or plant a few seeds, this gets checked off the list. In the studio, I throw the components of a piece and let them dry to the point where they can be assembled. Or I'll measure the chemicals for a glaze to be sieved and watered when time allows. I may wrap pots for shipping when I have a short break, then come back later in the day to place them in the box and create a shipping label.

When the children were young and at home, this strategy was indispensable, as I was always leaving the studio to take them to school, activities, and so on. My workflow became more manageable, and divvying up tasks this way allowed me to interweave being a parent and an artist. I did not have expectations for one long, uninterrupted spell spent in the studio, and yet, little by little, the pots were finished and the children grew up.

A Garden to Call My Own

From the beginning of my pottery career, I have documented my work in photographs. In this way, each piece has a "birth record" of sorts. And I realized early on that the best way to give a sense of scale to the work was to place flowers in the vases. This led me down the path of learning to garden in order to have special blooms expressly for the photos. Besides, getting my hands in the soil was not unlike the sensation of working with clay, and felt quite familiar and satisfying.

When Wally and I moved into our 1850s colonial house, I had the opportunity to plan a large cutting garden. The property is flat, with wonderful sun all day long. Everything I initially planted was selected for its suitability for photographs. Over the years, I learned which plants do well during a hot, humid Connecticut summer; if a flower has not functioned well, it's edited out and not replanted the following season.

The great twentieth-century English gardener Christopher Lloyd instructed that you should garden for yourself. This I absolutely do. My gardens are neither elegant perennial borders nor beautifully organized plots. Wally and I constructed a large, round garden when we moved to the property. We installed the simple, hand-built fence that remains in place twenty-five years later; four beds placed within it allow for planting in rows. Eventually, a decrepit and unused tennis court on the property, built in the 1930s, became a second garden. It now holds thirty raised beds devoted to flowers. The weathered, cracked asphalt provides excellent opportunities for volunteer plants to self-seed into the fissures. I won't win any garden design prizes for these spaces, but they produce an abundance of flowers, as well as ample herbs and tomatoes. Standing in either garden, which I do over many moments across the day, brings me joy. (I am convinced that if everyone grew flowers, the world would be a kinder place.) I love to share blossoms with family and friends so that they, too, can partake of the bounty.

When the dahlias are at their peak, as they were on this early October morning, I marvel to see the abundant colors and forms in the round cutting garden. The following pages offer a view of the same garden from the second floor of my studio

For the Love of Dahlias

Paging through a gardening book one day, I saw a bloodred dahlia for the first time and was instantly smitten. That same summer, our family visited Golden Gate Park in San Francisco, which has one of the great dahlia display gardens. The local dahlia society members who maintained the flowers were having their annual exhibition nearby. I was mesmerized and spent a lot of time discussing resources with the people tending the beds and exhibiting flowers. I asked them to recommend tuber suppliers, and I planned to order for the following summer. Thus began my long love affair.

In the 1990s, the dahlia was not considered chic, nor was it grown with the enthusiasm it is today. When I mentioned back then that I loved dahlias and was growing all sorts of colors and shapes, my gardener friends would roll their eyes. But I insisted—and still maintain—that the dahlia is an almost perfect flower. It starts blooming in midsummer and continues until frost. With a minimum of preparation, it will give bloom after bloom when most other plants have finished for the season. Its only slight failings are a lack of fragrance

and that if it is cut before the petals have unfurled, the bud will not open at all.

For a number of years, I have taught a class at the New York Botanical Garden on how to grow these beauties. The class begins with the history of dahlias (see page 134 for an abbreviated version) and a brief lesson in botany. Then I discuss how to plant and maintain dahlias over the growing season.

Though sometimes mistaken for bulbs, dahlias are technically tubers. Much like another commonly known tuber, the potato, their stems sprout directly from the "eyes" of the tuber. In the part of the country where I live, dahlias are dug up in fall and replanted in the ground in spring because they will not survive freezing winter temperatures.

Planting dahlias is another excellent example of the maxim "Begin as you mean to go on," in the sense that it is imperative to set up a support system when the tuber is planted. If everything is organized correctly at the outset, the thick stems will move up through the staking and flower splendidly. Pages 126 to 131 take you through the process, beginning in spring.

The ball dahlia is the easiest type to grow. It is a prolific bloomer and stores well over the winter. One can have an enormous variety of sizes and shapes in the garden concentrating on this classification alone. It's hard to go wrong with any combination.

DIVIDING THE TUBERS

The first step before planting overwintered tubers is to determine whether you want to divide them. (Note: Newly purchased tubers will not need to be divided.) Some growers, especially the professional companies, divide tubers in fall to generate new inventory. Since I grow dahlias for myself and fall is a busy work time, I divide my tubers in spring, if at all. When an older plant's clump of tubers is very large, I will break it into parts, either by simply pulling the clump to separate it or by slicing it into several sections with a sharp knife. Sometimes the tubers just fall apart themselves. If the clump is not too large, I don't divide it at all—this results in a vibrant, fast-growing group of stems. An older, undivided clump of tubers usually sprouts out of the ground faster and produces flowers sooner. Ultimately, however, there is no set rule. Do what works best for your garden.

I like to share extra tubers with friends but have learned to hold on to at least one section of a divided clump so that I don't inadvertently give away the flower cultivar completely. I have lost many special dahlias this way over time and (sadly) have been unable to replace them.

TAGGING

I attempt to tag new dahlia tubers when they arrive with Impress-O metal tags, on which I write the name of the tuber and the year of purchase. I say "attempt" because over the seasons, the tags and tubers do not always stay together accurately when stored. Thus I take tuber names and tags with a grain of salt and wait to see what actually flowers. I also try to tag each separated clump as I divide, though I often run out of time and the determination to do this consistently.

PLANTING, STAKING, AND CAGING

I put my dahlias in the ground anytime from late April to mid-May, depending on the weather in Connecticut that particular year. You want to be sure that hard frosts are over for the season and the ground has begun to warm. Some gardeners say to plant dahlias at the same time as tomatoes, but I tend to start a bit earlier.

There are many methods for staking dahlias. I use a straightforward (if not aesthetically beautiful) combination of tomato cages and wooden stakes to hold the stems upright as they grow. A row of holes is dug in the ground, sized to fit the tuber or tubers, then tomato cages and three stakes are placed around each hole. A tuber is put in the center of each of these supports, not too deep into the soil—just a few inches (about 5 cm). Otherwise, there is a chance that excessive moisture in the soil will cause rotting.

I leave space between the rows so there's room to plant spring bulbs in fall. Tulips, hyacinths, daffodils, and fritillaries come up and die back even while I am putting dahlia tubers into the ground. The same method can work for placing dahlias in a border: Just plant bulbs around the spot where the dahlia tuber will go in spring.

FERTILIZING

For many years, when I planted tubers (both old and new), I would put an organic mixture of two parts bonemeal to one part potash on top of the soil after the tubers were covered (any organic fertilizer that has a low nitrogen number such as 5-3-5 or 5-10-10 would work for this). Recently, my friend Charlie McCormick, who is a master dahlia grower, recommended that I spray liquid seaweed fertilizer that has a 2-3-1 ratio over the entire garden every two weeks. I've done this now for the past two years, and the dahlias have bloomed beautifully. Theoretically, if you have good, organic soil, the dahlias should do fine without these additions. If you have the wherewithal, however, it is advisable to make the effort to fertilize to ensure prolific blooming.

WATERING

Do not water the tubers when they are first planted—too much water will rot them. I usually hold off on watering until June. By then the plants have grown nicely out of the soil. When it comes time to water, do so early in the morning so that any moisture left on the flowers or leaves will quickly dry off in the sun.

CHECKING FOR GROWTH

One has to be patient and wait for the first leaves to emerge from the soil. The timing depends on whether the tuber is new or has been stored inside over the winter, because a stored tuber may sprout more vigorously and sooner. Many a time I've dug down into the soil to see how a tuber is coming along and snapped off the sprout just as it was about to break through the ground. After doing this once too often, I've learned to allow the plants to emerge at their own rate. If nothing is coming up out of the ground after four weeks, I check to see if the tuber has rotted or failed to grow.

PINCHING STEMS

When a stem with the first set of leaves springs out of the soil, wait for the first flower bud to form. Pinch out this first, center bud to encourage the stem to branch out and form multiple stems. I do this only once per plant. If the tuber is old and multiple branches spring out from the beginning, I leave it all alone.

BLOOMING

In Connecticut, dahlias start blooming by the third week in July. As each plant grows, I guide it through the tomato cage and use string as needed to keep the stems heading upward. The dahlia stem is hollow and stiff, and if one tries to move a stem that has grown along the ground, it will simply snap. If a stem needs tying up, make sure you have string and scissors at the ready so that the plant is moved around just once. This bit of attention at this early stage is important for the autumn harvest, because you want the plant to grow up straight and firm.

PINCHING BUDS

Dahlia flower buds often form in groups of three. Pinching out the two smaller side buds encourages the center bud to shoot up, and the flower will be larger. This creates a stronger, straighter stem for

cutting. But even if you don't pinch buds, the plant will continue to flower happily, albeit with smaller blossoms. It all comes down to how you want to spend your time and energy.

CUTTING

By the time September rolls around, the dahlias should be tall and in full bloom. I cut my flowers either early in the morning or late at night because it is cooler at these times. Cutting in the heat of the day stresses the flower immediately. I don't do anything special to the water in the bucket or vase, though some growers advise placing the stems in hot water to seal off the ends. Remember to let the flower open fully before cutting, as the bud will not open further once it is off the plant.

DIGGING UP THE TUBERS

Fast-forward to the first frost. We can have a frost in Connecticut anytime from mid-October to early November.

Sometimes the temperature dips just enough to freeze the dahlias, then rises again for several weeks. No matter: Once a strong cold has hit the plants, they are done for the year. The tubers should not be dug up, however, until there have been several strong frosts. This allows them to cure for hardiness. They then need to be removed before the ground freezes entirely. I usually lift my tubers in early November.

Saving tubers over the winter is not obligatory, of course. They can be purchased new each year, if you don't have the interest or ability to save them. Should you wish to do so, first remove whatever support system you devised in spring when they were planted. Using garden clippers, cut off the withered stems about 4 inches (10 cm) above the ground. Gently work around the perimeter of the plant with a shovel or pitchfork. The larger the plant, the farther out one should start feeling for the outer edge of the tubers. Inevitably,

some of the tubers will be snapped off when the plant is lifted out of the ground. These may be saved, depending on where the tuber is broken. If the plant has a name tag, place the tag immediately around where the stems meet the tuber, as later, the tubers will be impossible to identify. I do not wash my tubers; I simply shake off as much dirt as possible. As mentioned earlier, I don't divide the clumps at this stage.

STORING

I move my tubers in a wheelbarrow to the cement floor of my barn basement. I spread them out in one layer so that they can dry for a few days. Sometimes the length of the stems on the tuber clumps need to be trimmed to facilitate easy storage in boxes.

To store the tubers, I fill large cardboard boxes (the same ones I use to ship pots) with a combination of straw and wood shavings. (For years, I used peat moss, but this is no longer a sustainable option. The natural bogs and their ecosystems are fragile due to overharvesting.) I place the mixture on the bottom of the box and begin arranging the tubers, putting the largest clumps in first and filling in with the smallest at the top. The entire group of tubers is covered with the straw-and-shavings mixture, and the box is closed up.

The ideal storage temperature for the tubers is around 40°F (4.5°C). Sometimes my barn basement hovers just above freezing, but as long as the room does not actually dip below this

temperature, the tubers will be okay. It is better to have a colder room than one too warm. (A heated garage is not a good storage place for tubers.)

I learned the hard way not to store the boxes directly on the floor. We had a flood in the basement last year, and many of the old, large tubers on the bottom of the boxes got wet and rotted. I lost some of my best dahlias, ones that are difficult to replace. Now I store the boxes on wood two-by-fours to keep them just above the floor.

I do not check the boxes over the winter. There is something so rewarding and lovely about opening them in April to see how the tubers fared. Most of the time, they come through okay, last winter excepted. The tubers are like old friends, and knowing that we have all made it through the cold, dark months is a truly wonderful feeling. The promise of a new growing season fills me with great, enthusiastic anticipation.

Dahlias, Then and Now

The dahlia originated in Mexico, where it was planted in Aztec gardens. Francisco Hernández de Toledo, the personal physician to Spain's King Philip II, provided an early European record of the dahlia. He visited Mexico from 1570 to 1577 and described three species: *Dahlia pinnata*, *D. imperialis*, and *D. merckii*. In 1789, Antonio José Cavanilles, who worked at the Royal Botanical Garden in Madrid, received plants from the Botanical Garden of Mexico City.

Cavanilles mentioned three plants, *Dahlia pinnata*, *D. rosea*, and *D. coccinea*, and these were the beginning of the dahlia hybrids that number today in the thousands. (He named the plant "dahlia" after Andreas Dahl, a student of the Swedish botanist Carl Linnaeus, who had recently died.)

In 1798, Lady Bute, the wife of the English ambassador to the court of Spain, sent dahlia seeds to Kew Gardens, and in 1804, Alexander von Humboldt, the great German botanist and explorer, sent

September is prime time for the honeybees, which often sit for hours, even days, in the dahlias' open petals, lazily collecting pollen.

seeds from Mexico to Paris and Berlin. These seeds appear to have been cross-pollinated in Mexico before arriving and produced new single- and double-flowered dahlias.

The three different sources contributed to the dahlia's rapid spread across Europe in the early 1800s and to the subsequent dahlia craze, which caused growers to develop new shapes and colors.

SOURCING DAHLIAS

Since it was established in 1915, the American Dahlia Society has set the standard for exhibition blooms in the United States. Their handbook is a fascinating study of rules for competition and continues to inform and inspire amateur and professional growers. The Dahlia Society provides standardized information about size, shape, and color along with a list of classic cultivars. There are currently a vast number of new dahlia breeders, and the future classics remain to be seen.

With all the possibilities available these days, how does a new dahlia grower choose what to plant? I suggest you think in terms of color. If you love pink flowers, for example, then select plants of different sizes and shapes in a range of pink hues. All dahlia catalogs rate tubers for size, starting with the largest (AA, then A, B, BB, etc.), and for type (Decorative, Cactus, Ball, Water Lily, etc.); use this information to strategize a varied planting scheme.

The people I met at the San Francisco dahlia garden gave me a list of their favorite suppliers, and I began ordering from them right away. I was keen on bloodred dahlias and chose a variety of sizes and shapes. Over time, I moved away from the black reds, as they absorb too much light in front of a camera; lighter-colored dahlias are easier to photograph. Although many new farms with wonderful selections of tubers have sprung up recently, I gladly continue to support the first two growers I discovered, Ferncliff Gardens and Swan Island Dahlias (see Sources, page 242).

I am often asked why I order new tubers when I have hundreds boxed up. There are several reasons, the main one being that I am eager to try different shapes and colors, and suppliers offer new varieties each year. I reorder the classic forms as backup, in case the stored ones don't make it through winter. Some cultivars, like 'Café au Lait', don't like to be stored, so I purchase new tubers every year. I am on a constant quest for the most unusual dahlia blooms, heirlooms as well as standards, and I love to see how they change as the summer progresses. Late-in-the-season dahlias take on a different personality when the nights get cool, and I find these permutations most intriguing. It might fill a whole book if I were to catalog *all* the dahlias I've grown. What follows instead are examples of several of my favorites, showing the range of colors, shapes, and styles I plant in a given year.

'Walter Hardisty'
'Chilson's Pride'
Species dahlia

'Café au Lait'
'Lady Darlene'
'Meadowburn Clara Helen'

'Bracken Rose'
'Castle Drive'
'Rothesay Reveller'

'Heather Marie'
'Chimacum Davi'
'Meadowburn Byba Vincenza'

'Penhill Watermelon'
'Fuzzy Wuzzy'
'Ken's Choice'

'Sir Alfred Ramsey'
'Elsie Huston'
'Eagle's Sugar Plum'

'Myrtle's Brandy'
'Lake Ontario'
'Hollyhill Warlock'

'Jane Cowl'
'Honka'
'Hollyhill Dr. Rick'

'A la Mode'
'Ova Joxi'
'Juanita'

'Butterscotch'
'Wyn's Sundazzler'
'Zorro'

'AC Ben'
'Show 'n' Tell'
'Bishop of Llandaff'

'Clyde's Choice'
'Bodacious'
'Spartacus'

Great Inspirations

I adore the British garden sensibility and their collective ability to compose gardens full of exuberant blooms. Taken one by one, the flowers in these gardens give me tremendous inspiration for what to plant so that I can have beautiful stems for my vases. My favorite garden is Rousham in Oxfordshire, designed in the eighteenth century by William Kent. The landscape, for all that it is centuries old, feels very modern, with a sleek rill (narrow brook) that weaves through the property and ends at an elegant pond. There is also a vast cutting garden with old trees and splendid perennials. A few other British gardens follow close behind. Among them are Great Dixter, home of late gardener and gardening writer Christopher Lloyd, where flowers and shrubs are composed and planted as if part of a large symphony; Sissinghurst, designed by Vita Sackville-West in the 1930s, which is famous for its rooms of flowers by color and season; and the cutting garden at Charleston, once the country home of Bloomsbury group artists Vanessa Bell and Duncan Grant and their family.

There are so many gardens in the United Kingdom that I have yet to see, but I have numerous books for reference. These allow me to study the entire growing season rather than simply what's in bloom when I happen to visit. I am very glad to have seen the gardens at

Hadspen House in 1998, since they no longer exist. The owners, Sandra and Nori Pope, wrote a wonderful book documenting their now-vanished garden; their instruction, including information on individual plant selection, remains enormously helpful.

That being said, there are spectacular gardens closer to home as well. I have been involved for many years with Wave Hill, an exquisite gem in the Bronx, New York. The grounds are designed with different rooms that bloom stupendously each season. Wave Hill is open year-round, and the Gardener's Party, held every September, is not to be missed. I am a member of their Friends of Horticulture committee—there is nothing better than being in a room with fellow plant lovers. I enjoy making trips to the New York Botanical Garden in the Bronx as well. It is like taking a trip around the world thanks to the garden's different landscapes and greenhouses.

The Garden Conservancy is a national organization that lists gardens both large and small throughout the United States that are open to the public. I have participated in their Open Days program, whereby members invite visitors to tour their personal gardens. Held from early spring well into the fall, these events provide an excellent opportunity to learn and get new ideas from local gardeners.

I have been collecting bearded irises for a number of years but am even more enthusiastic after learning about Cedric Morris, the English painter who in the 1950s bred them for his garden and his art. They have been recently revived in the United Kingdom.

My Planting Strategy

The dahlia is the queen of my garden, but I love all flowers. I like to choose a broad selection of shapes and colors within a specific flower family, from amaranth to zinnias, studying each variety's provenance and the best ways to cultivate it. This gives me options when arranging a bouquet. Each year, I add something new. I recently tried heirloom chrysanthemums, which were fantastic. I will plant loads of them again, along with a few new (to me) cultivars of gladioli, bearded iris, and roses.

A cutting garden can be created without a greenhouse or a place to start seedlings. Since I don't have a greenhouse (though one is currently in the works) or the time to set up a seed-sprouting arrangement, I opt for the most straightforward way to grow flowers: directly sowing seeds, planting bulbs, and purchasing transplants. I plant both annuals and perennials; some perennials (such as peonies) take a number of years before they reach maturity, so I have to patiently wait for their beautiful blooms.

I plan a continual bloom sequence, from the earliest snowdrops to the last dahlias and chrysanthemums. Tubers and corms are easy to plant; one just needs to allow time (maybe years) for the plants to mature. There is a wonderful organic farmer near my town who grows flowers as plugs (small plants in cells) that can be ordered in January and collected in May. I allow for a certain amount of sprouting failure and try to have backup plants if the first round is not successful.

Strategizing which flowers to plant and when is a year-round proposition. Because gardening is fashionable now and more people are purchasing seeds and tubers with great enthusiasm, suppliers make their stock available increasingly earlier in the year. One has to be mindful of release dates from some of the smaller and more eccentric suppliers to avoid missing out. The best time to order dahlia tubers to plant the following spring, for example, may be August or September, depending on the company. Spring bulbs, including tulips, narcissus, muscari, and hyacinth, can be selected in July. Seed companies still largely release their new catalogs in early January, timed to entice the gardener in the midst of a long, dreary winter. I find myself repeating the phrase "Hope springs eternal" as packet after packet gets put into the virtual shopping cart along with dreams of splendid bouquets.

In November, I plant tulips, daffodils, and other spring-blooming bulbs in rows in between the places where I will set tomato cages for the dahlia tubers the following April (see page 127). Then, when these spring bulbs are blooming, I can slip the dahlias into the ground, and they will begin to sprout just as the bulbs' flowers are fading away.

Spring Bounty

My original goal for the cutting garden was to grow varieties that weren't sold at flower markets. Since then, I have made selections based on what would look most interesting (and beautiful) in my photographs.

Now that there are more heirloom and other rare flowers available for growing, I'm able to go deep within favorite types. I've lost some of the cultivar names over the years, or failed to remember the names of plants my gardener friends have given me. The names are not as important to me as the flowers' reappearance each year, however. On the following pages are many of my most reliable spring blooms, all of which add to the splendid chaos of the season.

Below: I am most fond of fragrant narcissi, including the delicate early-blooming yellow *Narcissus* 'Rapture', the white double-petaled *N.* 'White Medal', the orange-centered *N.* 'Barrett Browning', and the pheasant's eye narcissus (*N. poeticus* var. *recurvus*) with its red-edged center.

Opposite: Among the tulips I grow are the scarlet lily-flowered *Tulipa* 'Ballerina' and lily-flowered 'White Triumphator'; maroon-and-yellow 'Gavota'; brilliant red double-form 'Miranda'; 'Orange Emperor', 'Rembrandt', and 'Salmon Impression'; and peony-flowering 'Black Hero', 'La Belle Époque', and 'Orange Princess'.

Opposite: Muscari, also known as blue grape hyacinth, have the most magical florets and come in all shades of blue and purple. My go-tos include *Muscari armeniacum* (the most commonly found bulb); the pale blue *M. armeniacum* 'Valerie Finnis'; *M. paradoxum*, which is a deep shade of blue with yellow outlines on the edges; and *M. latifolium* with its deep blue florets, topped off with a paler blue hat.

Right: I usually spread poppy seeds in the cold of February for the best crop. These include Shirley poppies (*Papaver rhoeas*): delicate white and white with pink edges 'Angel's Choir'; variegated pink, red, and white 'Falling in Love'; deep crimson 'Legion of Honor'; and multihued 'Mother of Pearl'. The dark purple is *P. somniferum* 'Lauren's Grape'. I also adore the frilly breadseed poppies, including *P.* 'Pink Peony'.

Left: The pale blue bearded iris was a gift from my sister-in-law's garden in Napa, California; I believe it is 'Victoria Falls'. I purchased the deep orange iris, 'Avalon Sunset', from Piet Oudolf's gardens at the Battery Park Conservancy in New York City a number of years ago. The mocha and cream–colored iris is 'Champagne Elegance', the black is 'Hello Darkness', the white is 'Angelwalker', and the burgundy and peach is 'Action Packed'.

Opposite: Friends gave me my peonies without specific identifications, except for the white 'Festiva Maxima'. Here are varieties that are close to what I have in the garden: The soft pink peonies are similar to 'Sarah Bernhardt', 'Nick Shaylor', 'Mrs. Franklin D. Roosevelt', and 'Lady Alexandra Duff'. The dark colors resemble 'Red Charm' and 'Big Ben'.

ROASTED TOMATO SAUCE

Tomatoes are among the only edibles that merit space in my flower garden. Every spring, I plant a number of the long San Marzanos as well as cherry tomatoes, Sungolds, and other varieties; now there are many lovely cultivars that are especially suitable for cooking. My tomato crop is better some years than others. If I don't have a good harvest, I go to the farmers' market or a nearby farm stand and purchase tomatoes. At the end of summer, I make a large quantity of sauce to use during the winter months. The sauce is essential for any number of recipes that I put together, such as beef stew, pizzas, pastas, and soups. Most important, the taste instantly brings back the memory of late summer and fall, which is consoling during the cold, dark evenings of January and February. Several batches of sauce should last until the following spring, about six months. *Makes approximately 1 quart (950 ml)*

3 pounds (1.3 kg) tomatoes
5 garlic cloves
¼ cup (60 ml) olive oil
1 tablespoon (15 g) kosher salt
½ teaspoon red pepper flakes
Mixed fresh herbs, such as rosemary, thyme,
   and basil

SPECIAL EQUIPMENT
Food mill

Preheat the oven to 400°F (205°C).

Spread the tomatoes and garlic in a small roasting pan or shallow ovenproof dish. Pour the olive oil over them, then sprinkle with the salt and red pepper flakes. Scatter the fresh herbs over the top. Roast for 1½ to 2 hours, or until the tomatoes begin to collapse and the tops are a nice blackened brown. Let the tomatoes cool until they are at room temperature.

Place a food mill on top of a large bowl. Scrape everything from the roasting pan— tomatoes, garlic, herbs, and all the juices—into the mill and purée the mixture into the bowl. If the sauce seems a bit thin, transfer it to a large pot and cook over medium-low heat for a couple of hours, stirring occasionally with a wooden spoon. After the sauce has thickened to the desired consistency, let it cool completely, then pour it into plastic containers or freezer bags and freeze for up to 6 months.

Embracing the Random

Though I sketch designs before sitting at the wheel, the throwing does not always go according to plan. Nevertheless, over the years, I've learned to see each pot through to completion; whatever the result of the throwing, it gets trimmed, fired, and glazed. I don't consider any outcome a failure (or "second"). Either the pot has some redeeming aspect and can be kept or offered for sale, or I have learned something from its faults to apply going forward. I have come to appreciate the slight, often subtle differences in each piece as inherent to the value of my work. In fact, I believe that this unpredictability is the key to my fascination with ceramics and propels my desire to keep working. Something unexpected always arises, which (usually) delights me and (hopefully) sustains my interest.

Years ago, my friend the photographer Marion Brenner pitched a story on my work to *House & Garden* magazine. The plan was for her and an editor (Stephen Orr, who became a new friend) to visit my studio. Together we would select flowers from my garden to arrange in one of my pots. I remember working late on a Saturday evening to finish some pieces in time. As I was moving away from the wheel, I accidentally knocked over a large-belly pot before it was attached to the pedestal and rim. The shape on the floor was now a flattened oval, but as I didn't want to lose momentum, I decided to adapt to the change. I threw a wide

rim and made both it and the foot an oval shape. I heavily fluted these parts and added curvilinear handles, then I placed the pot on top of a firing kiln to dry.

We ended up using the finished piece in the shoot, filling it with exuberant sunflowers in bloom. The effect—and the photograph—was pure magic. It was chosen for the magazine's cover, and the pot was purchased by editor in chief Dominique Browning. The experience was a great lesson in adapting to circumstances and learning to turn a potential failure into something positive.

The same sorts of happy accidents occur in the garden. There I've learned to eagerly anticipate the volunteer seedlings that pop up from the previous year's flowers. I never know beforehand where they will emerge; each spring, it's thrilling to recognize an errant poppy, sunflower, calendula, or amaranth leaf.

Usually, the seeds that survive the cold winter months are the most vigorous and eventually produce the tallest plants. I am grateful for their contribution to the garden landscape as it unfolds and to the arrangements of cut flowers they help me compose. Volunteer sunflowers often grow 14 feet (over 4 m) high, with thick, fibrous stems. Amaranth produces literally hundreds of seedlings and is especially welcome in summer and autumn arrangements mixed with dahlias. Unplanned flowers are gifts, and I let them flourish wherever they wish.

Opposite: When I see this shot, which graced the cover of *House & Garden* magazine, I am reminded of making the pot and how important it is to see an idea through to the end.

Following pages: The tennis court garden is home to many dozens of dahlia varieties as well as a host of volunteers, whose seeds fill in and sprout from cracks in the ground or bare spots in the raised beds.

Making Flower Molds, Step-by-Step

I can't remember exactly when I began making plaster casts of my garden flowers, but it must have been close to twenty years ago. My favorite casts capture the essence of summer and fall flowers long after they're gone. Pushing clay into these forms results in near-perfect ceramic replicas that I then apply to ceramic pots. People often wonder how the applied-clay pieces can be so exact to the flower yet still somehow not; it's because the clay transforms in shape while it is fired and glazed.

Mixing plaster is not a perfect science, and all the materials must be organized before the process begins: To start, cut the sides of an empty cardboard box to about 3 inches (7.5 cm) high. Mark about 2 inches (5 cm) up the sides of the box to indicate the level to which the plaster should be poured. Cover the bottom seams and side joints of the box with packing tape, to prevent the wet plaster from seeping through any open spaces. Place two large buckets side by side. Then (while wearing plastic gloves—plaster is caustic and can burn your skin—and a face mask) weigh out the dry plaster in one and measure the water in the other, following the

guidelines on the container. Next, go out to the garden to pick the flowers to be cast. Some flowers are more conducive to plaster casting than others; smaller dahlias, zinnias, cosmos, and anemone work well. I try to pick a range of sizes and shapes. It's best to pick the flowers just before casting so that the shapes are firm and fresh. Cut the stems 2 to 3 inches (5 to 7.5 cm) long. Then it's time to begin making your cast.

1. Lay the flowers on paper near the two buckets. The process goes very quickly, so you want the flowers close at hand for placing in the wet plaster. Wearing gloves, slowly sprinkle handfuls of plaster into the water and wait for the last handful to be absorbed. Using a drill with a plastic mixing end, mix the plaster and water for 2 to 3 minutes. You want the plaster the consistency of light cream—not too thin but not too thick.

2. Immediately pour the plaster into the cardboard box.

3. Working quickly, place the flower heads facedown in the wet plaster. Do not move them once you have immersed them in the plaster. Fill in the sheet with flowers, leaving about ½ inch (1 cm) between the blooms.

4. After about 30 minutes, begin to pull the flowers out of the plaster and peel away the cardboard. (Don't worry if a few petals remain stuck in the plaster—they will eventually dry and flake off.) The plaster plaque will get warm as it sets—this is how plaster hardens. It takes a few weeks for the plaster cast to dry completely before you can use it. If the days are still warm, set the cast outside in the sun to speed up the curing.

I employ pressed
flowers in various
ways on my pots.
When placed all
over the body of a
piece and at times
overlapping, as they
are on this round
vase, they become
sculptural. Arranged
in more orderly
rows, as around the
edge of the pedestal
bowl opposite, the
flowers resemble
medallions, in a nod
to neoclassicism.

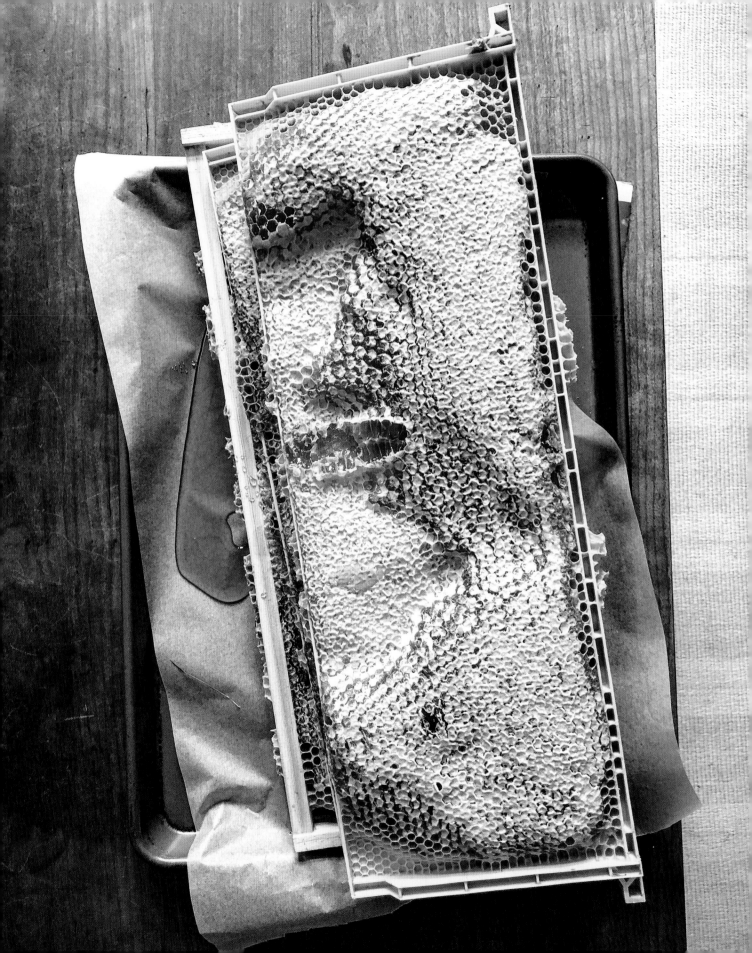

Beekeeping

Several years ago, I started keeping European honeybees at one end of my tennis-court garden. I was interested in promoting flower pollination, and also intrigued by the age-old practice of beekeeping. (Bees have been on the planet from the beginning, some forty million years ago.) Much like my other vocations—making ceramics, gardening, and cooking—there is a classical reference to apiarian work that appeals to me, and a natural symbiosis between them all. The bees pollinate the flowers, which later fill the vases and bowls. And like those other processes, beekeeping requires study, discipline, and a fair amount of dedication. Yet it can't be controlled entirely; variables keep the practice unpredictable and therefore interesting. Beekeeping remains something of an intellectual challenge, too, which I love.

To get me started, a local beekeeper set me up with two hives, and she taught me the fundamentals. When she moved away, I had to care for the bees without her guidance. (Luckily, Victor Schrager, an accomplished photographer and friend, has been keeping bees for years and is always up for discussing all things bee-related.)

I check the hives regularly, looking for larvae to make sure the queen is laying her eggs. I use a smoker when I inspect the bees, as the smoke interferes with their sense of smell, which is used to alert the other bees of potential threats to the hive. I love the fragrance of the smoke and how it lingers after I am done inspecting. To combat varroa mites, the most destructive enemy of the beehive, I use formic acid strips, which contain an organic miticide, twice a year and a different preventive solution in early January. I make sugar fondant cakes to lay across the top of the hives in winter, and when there isn't enough pollen, I'll make a thick sugar syrup for the bees so that they have additional food. Ultimately, I feel that no matter what I do, the bees will survive or not on their own. I am dedicated to their maintenance nonetheless.

Beekeeping is a metaphor for so much of what I do. When I'm calm, the bees are calm. They sense my mood, which keeps me in check. This parallels working with clay, which I do best when I have no distractions and can focus quietly in the studio. Also, the bees love the flowers in the garden, and I am happy to provide pollen for them to collect, keeping everything interwoven.

The greatest by-product of keeping bees is, of course, honey. I harvest four frames at a time, putting them into a machine that uses centrifugal force to extract the honey. Each batch tastes slightly different, due to any number of variables (including the time of year), and I look forward to dividing it among jars for friends and neighbors.

I am often struck by the parallels between the bees and my flowers, and how nature connects them in a grand scheme. The color and movement of the hive is echoed in the chrysanthemums' soft, folding, intricate petals. Many parts contribute to the whole.

HONEY–PEACH PRESERVES

An orchard of young fruit trees grows by my tennis-court garden, and the peach tree there yields a respectable harvest. Each year I make a small batch of peach jam flavored with the honey I collect from the nearby bees. The jam is not cloying, and the flavor of the peaches is predominant. *Makes approximately 2½ pints (1 L)*

> 20 to 25 medium peaches
> 1 to 1½ cups (240 to 360 ml) honey
> ⅓ cup (80 ml) lemon juice
>
> SPECIAL EQUIPMENT
> 5 or 6 half-pint (240 ml) sterilized canning jars
>   with lids, kept warm
> Boiling-water canner

Bring a large pot of water to a boil. Cut an X in the bottom of each peach and blanch them in boiling water for 2 to 3 minutes, or until you can easily remove the skins.

Remove the skins and pits, then chop the peaches into small chunks.

Transfer the chopped peaches to another large pot, then stir in the honey and lemon juice. Bring to a boil, then cook, stirring frequently, for 30 to 40 minutes, until the mixture has reached a jammy thickness.

Immediately pour or ladle the jam into the hot, sterilized jars, leaving ½ inch (1.5 cm) of headspace. Wipe the rims clean and carefully attach the lids. Follow the boiling-water-canning procedure (see the USDA guidelines at nchfp.uga.edu) to process the jars for 10 minutes, adjusting for altitude as needed per USDA guidelines.

Books, My Constant Companions

I never know where an idea will come from, and I remain open to all possibilities. Books are a key element of this endeavor.

I often bring books home after I visit an art exhibition or when I travel to a new place and want to be reminded of a particular feeling or mood. Sometimes when I can't attend an art show, I will order the exhibition catalog (it's much cheaper than a plane ticket).

Because I live in the suburbs and there aren't many bookstores left, sadly, I tend to buy books online. Almost daily, a stream of books arrives at the studio. This gives me something to look forward to, but it also presents a challenge, since I need to make space for the new volumes that come in. Some people might think it's extravagant to buy so many books, but if I find even one good idea, I consider the purchase worthwhile. Rarely do I get just one idea, though. Usually, I revisit a book over and over and discover something completely new each time I read it.

When I was about ten, my mother gave me huge tomes on Leonardo da Vinci, Rembrandt, and Michelangelo that still sit on my shelves today. She encouraged me to keep reading and collecting. I've since built an excellent resource library that I continually reference. I focus on ceramics, art history, design, photography, gardening, botanical drawing, and cooking. My abundance of gardening books has helped me survive more than thirty long Connecticut winters and taught me most of what I know about plants and flowers. The same holds true for cooking and baking. I learned about cakes, pies, cookies, and more by working my way through several wonderful old cookbooks.

When it comes to my art books, I am drawn to certain overall themes: tonality, texture, composition, balance, framing, and imperfection. Reading, referencing, and looking at images stirs up ideas and can lead to new series of pots, new plants for the garden, or innovative ways to photograph the flowers. It is part of my investment in the design process and what makes me excited to go to work each day.

I love to gather a pile of books on one topic—cutting gardens, for instance—to research how to proceed with my own project. I gather from each book the bits that pertain to whatever it is I am trying to create. This is not dissimilar to my approach to planting flowers: I have a large selection, and I pick what moves me. There is choice and abundance in a good way, and something new and exciting inevitably happens.

I reference a rotating stack of books as I am sketching shapes to throw. The challenge is to keep the books free from clay as, inevitably, I reach for one while I am at the wheel (as you can see from the smudges on the well-worn Lucie Rie catalog, a particular favorite, at the top of this stack).

LUCIE RIE

LUCIE RIE

craftscouncil

THE ARNHOLD COLLECTION OF MEISSEN PORCELAIN 1710–50   Cassidy-Geiger   Kuhn   Biedermann   THE FRICK COLLECTION   9

R

Erickson   ROYAL DELFT A Guide to *De Porceleyne Fles*   Schiffer

GIACOMETTI ET LES ÉTRUSQUES

Los Jarrones de la Alhambra   SIMBOLOGÍA Y PODER

Arte islámico en Granada · Propuesta para un Museo de la Alhambra

DATE-NUT BREAD

A few well-known cooks and bakers inspire my time in the kitchen. I read their books to get ideas about composing a menu or baking. I turn to Maida Heatter's cookbooks often. Her recipes strike the perfect balance of flavors and texture. The date-nut bread from her *New Book of Great Desserts*, which I've adapted here, is a staple in our house. I have been making it for more than thirty years, and it is delicious topped with honey-peach preserves (see page 165). *Makes 1 loaf*

8 tablespoons (1 stick/113 g) unsalted butter, at room temperature, plus more for the pan

1⅓ cups (165 g) all-purpose flour, plus more for the pan

1 cup (125 g) pitted dates

1 cup (145 g) raisins (light or dark or a combination)

1 teaspoon baking soda

1 cup (240 ml) boiling water

1 teaspoon vanilla extract

1 cup (200 g) sugar

¼ teaspoon salt

½ teaspoon instant espresso powder

1 large egg

1¾ cups (166 g) walnut or pecan halves

Preheat the oven to 350°F (180°C). Butter a 9-by-5-inch (2.3-by-13 cm) loaf pan and dust with flour.

Cut the dates into medium-size pieces and place with raisins in a mixing bowl. Dissolve the baking soda in the boiling water and pour over the raisins and dates.

In a large bowl, cream the butter with a mixer. Add the vanilla, sugar, salt, and espresso powder and beat well. Beat in the egg. Add the flour and beat just until incorporated.

Stir in some of the liquid from the date mixture, then stir in all the dates, raisins, and their liquid. Stir in the nuts. Pour the batter into the pan and smooth the top.

Maida says to bake the loaf for 1½ hours, but I usually pull it out of the oven at 1 hour 10 minutes. The bread will get quite dark. Transfer the pan to a wire rack to allow the bread to cool before turning it out of the pan. Let cool completely before serving.

Being a Work-at-Home Parent

I had one child and was pregnant with my second when I started making ceramics. It never occurred to me to stop working while the children were small. Even after I had my third child, I continued to grow my business. I would hire a babysitter a couple of mornings a week, or I'd work when the kids were napping. Sometimes they played alongside me as I completed some aspect of the job.

Making potato-stamp prints with them in the kitchen one day, I devised the pot chop that I have used as my trademark for the pots ever since. Looking back, this is a good example of how seamlessly my roles as mother and businessperson were intertwined. I did not have a grand plan for motherhood or for my pottery, but I never doubted that I would do both simultaneously, somehow figuring it out as I went along.

People have told me that they used to make art but stopped once they had children. I find this difficult to comprehend. Why eliminate a source of such creativity and joy? Having work that I was passionate about was important to my experience of parenting. My children saw that I was involved in activities independent of them, and they were completely supportive. Pursuing my career also served as a model for what it meant to be dedicated to a job and, at the same time, to one's family.

I treated my kids as I treat everyone—with consideration—and in turn, they learned to respect others, including their parents (most of the time, anyway!). I remember moments when I was tired and they were demanding. We were all cranky. I would remind them that I am a person, too, with the same feelings they have, and not just their mother. Then we each took a deep breath. That message seemed to resonate with them, and to give us all some perspective.

Now even though they are far from home, we have good communication. I serve as a sounding board for their own struggles with work and home and how best to balance the two.

I made my original potato print stamp in a notebook many years ago. It has since been adapted for my logo and branding, as well as for the pot chop on my porcelain work.

FRANCES
PALMER
POTTERY

FRANCES PALMER®
POTTERY

ON GATHERING MY TRIBE

When I was in high school, I would come home some afternoons to find my mother and a few of her friends playing cards. I did not particularly relate to them, and I told myself that if I ever had a daughter, I would introduce her to artistic, accomplished women. Fast-forward to the birth of my daughter when I turned thirty, and I had not forgotten my goal.

When asked to name some of my heroes, I think of all of my female friends who work hard and do beautiful things. My daughter, Daphne, grew up with many "other mothers," and I feel fortunate that she has women whom she can rely on, in addition to me. She got married a few summers ago at the home of her biggest champion, her aunt Pamela (Wally's sister). With so many of Daphne's fairy godmothers in the room, I gave a toast in which I remarked that she is a splendid person herself due in no small part to all the people who helped raise her. I also thanked the same women on behalf of my two sons, who benefited from being around these fantastic role models.

These friends make up a huge support system. As much as I love my family, there is no substitute for having another woman to talk to about anxieties, fears, triumphs, tribulations, and the day-to-day job of being female. I recently hosted a group of close friends for a darning and mending day in my studio. It was a lively group of like-minded, creative women—gardeners, writers, painters, potters, photographers, knitters, and crafters among them. Most of them were true multi-hyphenates, able to claim several such titles at once. Some guests knitted while others darned and repaired clothing. We enjoyed an afternoon of spirited conversation and camaraderie, and the effect was a combination of therapy and growth.

I also enjoy meeting up with a smaller group for an expedition to a museum or lecture as often as my schedule allows. It is a gift to find a circle of artist friends, with whom I can share, explore, and cross-pollinate ideas.

PERFECT ROAST CHICKEN

Every November, I have an open studio day. For many years, I would invite
twenty to thirty women to stay for a meal after the sale. That was the beginning
of the "Ladies' Dinner" tradition. I usually made roast chickens, and many of the
guests brought dishes as well, for a great potluck. I think often of the crescendo
of voices in the dining room as the conversation waxed glorious. It made me
feel wonderful to assemble such an incredible group of women in one room,
year after year. *Serves 4*

One 3½- to 4-pound (1.6 to 1.8 kg) chicken
Kosher salt and freshly ground pepper
Handful of fresh herbs, such as sage, thyme,
    rosemary, basil, and/or tarragon
1 lemon, cut in half
3 garlic cloves
3 tablespoons (42 g) butter
1 pear, apple, or peach, halved (optional)
Paprika

4 baking potatoes or sweet potatoes,
    peeled and chopped into large chunks
2 large onions, peeled and cut into quarters
Seasonal vegetables, such as carrots,
    fennel, butternut squash, mushrooms,
    Brussels sprouts, or zucchini, peeled and
    chopped into evenly sized pieces
Olive oil

Preheat the oven to 400°F (205°C).

Pat the chicken dry inside and out with a paper towel. Sprinkle salt and pepper
inside the cavity, then fill with the fresh herbs, one lemon half, the garlic cloves,
and 1 tablespoon (14 g) of the butter. (Sometimes I halve a piece of fruit, such as
a pear, apple, or peach, and put it in the cavity as well.)

Turn the chicken breast side down and sprinkle the bottom and sides with salt,
pepper, and paprika. Turn the chicken right side up and sprinkle the entire breast
and legs with salt, pepper, and paprika. Tie the legs together with kitchen twine.
Rub the remaining 2 tablespoons (28 g) butter on top of the bird, then put it breast
side up in a 10-inch (25 cm) cast-iron skillet.

Nestle the potatoes, onions, and vegetables around the chicken in the skillet. Pour a
bit of olive oil over the vegetables and sprinkle with salt and pepper.

Slide the skillet into the oven and roast, untouched, for 2 hours, or until a thermometer
inserted into the center registers 165°F (74°C), the juices run clear, and the leg
separates easily from the breast.

Pour off the excess fat, if desired, and serve the chicken and vegetables together
with the juices from the bottom of the skillet. Save all leftover bones and vegetables
to make a beautiful stock.

There's Nothing Like a Deadline

The question I am most frequently asked about my work is "How do you get it all done?" The answer is simple: There's nothing like a deadline. Not only am I always grateful to be given one, I simply don't work well without one. A deadline provides a known quantity of time in which to plan my production and work toward its completion. All of my orders have a due-by date to a certain extent; however, when a customer says a pot is needed by a birthday, or there is a specific installation date, I must adhere to it. When I have a trunk show or other sale on the calendar, suddenly my pace is ramped up. Any tendency to put one project ahead of another because it is simpler or more appealing is not an option. A short production window is the best kind of parameter; the sense of urgency sharpens my focus tremendously.

The best trick I've developed to cope with big deadlines is listening to audiobooks while I work. When a large order comes in, I download an audiobook, usually a lengthy work of fiction or a biography, to distract me from the looming date on the calendar. Listening to these spoken volumes helps me focus on the work and take it piece by piece. When I'm especially stressed about an order, I turn to Dickens, and everything always seems to turn out okay. I just finished listening to *Bleak House* for the umpteenth time. Even when I know the ending, audiobooks motivate me to keep working. In fact, when I'm working and listening at the same time, knowing the ending helps me enormously. I can't handle the suspense of not knowing how a story will end while also producing something unpredictable. There is great comfort in knowing how at least one of the two will turn out!

There is also a wonderful sense of accomplishment when the deadline is met and the event or project was a success. Rather than have pots head out the door with little fanfare, the big push to finish on time can bring a welcome kind of exhaustion. Before long, however, it's on to the next order and a new opportunity for fulfillment.

Prior to leaving for a week's trip away from the studio, I was determined to finish outstanding orders and get them packed and shipped. I left these boxes at the door, ready to be collected, then sailed away with a clear mind.

PART III

LOOKING FORWARD

Some days, I would like to spend hours throwing whatever I please or experimenting with glazes and forms, setting aside client commissions. That being said, customer requests are often what propel me into different directions and stretch my ideas. I might consider a shape in a book or museum that I'd like to explore, or conjure an idea for a vase that would be useful for flowers currently blooming in the garden—these things are among the many catalysts for new designs.

Evolution and growth are essential to any creative career. Documentation and record keeping and continual self-assessment of where my work has been and where it is headed both play a role in that progression. You have to look back to move forward, in some regard. I may rely on my available catalog to fulfill customer expectations and desires, but I always believe that the next group of work or the next firing is going to be the best articulation of my ideas. I feel that I have yet to throw the definitive form or achieve another of the elusive, gorgeous glazes that have captivated my attention for so long.

Open Studio

I started having studio sales sometime around 1994, in the fall. Wally and I had just moved to the colonial house, and I set up tables in the living room. I put out as much work as I could produce, unsure if this was the best strategy or, frankly, if anyone would show up. I photographed the pots, made a postcard, and mailed it to everyone I could think of, with personal messages to editors and clients.

The sale went well, and I found selling directly to customers much simpler than working with retail stores. I decided to have another go at it, and the following spring I hosted a second pot sale, this time out on the lawn. Although there was a good turnout, I decided that limiting it to one open studio per year made the event more special. I focused on building inventory for the fall.

The first weekend in November has proven to be the best time for the sale. It's close to the holiday season but not too near Thanksgiving, when the schedule gets more packed and the pace more frenetic. I don't send out postcards any longer. Email and social media updates are the most effective ways to announce the event, though I do miss having the physical notice and the ritual of something going out through the post.

It all seems straightforward now, but in the beginning I felt terribly vulnerable presenting my work and hoping the event would be well attended. It took years before the anxiety would abate and I would be happy to see friends and customers again, regardless of sales.

I used to refer to the event as my "pot sale," but that name is a misnomer, as I don't usually have a lot of work "on sale" with reduced prices. It is really an opportunity for customers to see work that is not online and perhaps more unexpected. The past few Novembers, I have called it an open studio so that people have different expectations about the day.

On the morning of a recent open studio, the second floor of the barn was filled with new pots. Customers were happy to see the work firsthand, and because there are often multiple versions of the same shape, it allowed them to understand the one-of-a-kind nature of each pot.

The Importance of Collaboration

I am primarily self-reliant as a businessperson, but obviously, that's not the entire picture. Though I am a company of one, that doesn't mean I always work alone. I have partners and collaborators in all facets of my work and at different levels of involvement.

Twice I have reached out to commercial manufacturing companies to produce a hand-cast dishware collection, and both of these partnerships have relied on mutual trust, integrity, and a shared vision. In 2005, I started a business with Niagara Ceramics in Buffalo, New York; together, we produced a collection of tableware to sell around the country. It was wonderful to work with a manufacturer so connected to the history of American factories. Sadly, it closed in 2013, and that was the end of an era. I searched for a new company to work with but did not see any viable options in the United States. I discovered the avant-garde factory 1882 Ltd., which is based in Stoke-on-Trent, England, and is continuing the great British creamware manufacturing tradition. I designed a small group of dishware made from my original shapes, and it is wonderful to be part of their operation.

In contrast, collaborations involving my handmade work often tap into different dimensions of the pottery. In 2014, florist Emily Thompson and I planned an opening in her shop with her fantastic arrangements of flowers and branches wrapped around and in dramatic vases and tulipieres with gold luster painting (as shown on the following pages). More recently, I invited Emily to conduct a dahlia workshop in my studio along with Charlie McCormick, a garden designer who lives in England. I was happy to partner with Emily and Charlie and to open the garden and studio to other dahlia enthusiasts. I've also hosted paper flower–making workshops with Livia Cetti of the Green Vase in my studio. Having the opportunity to understand other artists' approaches to their making is a great benefit of collaborations, as are the inevitable challenges and resultant new ideas.

Of course, no partnership has been as lasting or rewarding as the one I've shared with Wally. He has supported my work unfailingly, from the earliest days of the pottery business (and my knitwear business, which brought us together). This has given me the freedom to build the company I wanted. He remains a great confidant for much of what I do, knowing when to give advice (and just as important, when not to!). I deeply appreciate not only Wally's encouragement but also his respect for my most pronounced need: a fair amount of independence.

Opposite: These pieces were commissioned by Jenah Barry for the Fotografiska New York museum. I was glad to work on such a grand scale (each pot is 3 feet/about 1 meter tall; the model is on the bottom left). When placed in the windows and filled with branches and flowers, they couldn't be missed.

Following pages: The gold-accented pots were designed for Emily Thompson, and the lamps with Chad Jacobs of Bone Simple. I made the two vases with molded flower details for Philip Johnson's Glass House shop. Mieke ten Have commissioned the painted pitcher, and Aerin Lauder, the fluted cylinder vases. I designed the black lidded box, green striped vessels, and pots with cutwork detailing for the Neue Galerie shop ; the white vase (with tiny handles) was for Moda Operandi. The stacked dinnerware is from my Cirrus collection, in partnership with 1882 Ltd.

Arranging a Bouquet, Step-by-Step

In 2015, I took a flower workshop with Erin Benzakein of Floret Flowers, in the Skagit Valley of Washington State, and this expanded my comprehension of what could be part of a bouquet. Erin cut all sorts of trees, shrubs, and branches— the kind I had on my property, though I had not considered including them with flowers specifically grown for cutting.

A few years prior to my workshop with Erin, I met and became great friends with Amy Merrick, who at that time was on the crest of the new wave of floral designers working in Brooklyn, New York. She has since become a world traveler, bringing together many cultural ideas about arranging. Amy has an original and inventive approach to interweaving cut flowers and foraged material, and I learn something new each time she roams my flower beds.

I have also visited the pollinator garden at the Sakonnet Garden in Little Compton, Rhode Island, and learned that many of the plants I considered weeds were actually vital flowers for bees and butterflies. As a result of these connections, just about everything in my own garden is left to grow these days, and the bouquets are the richer for it.

My flower arrangements all begin the same way—with a trip to the garden at dawn. I walk among the flowers to see if a pattern of color, scale, or form or another unifying theme emerges to inspire my cutting. If I have a new vase that I wish to feature, I select plant material that will best complement its form. I always look for opportunities to add texture. Goldenrod, for

example, is considered a weed by some but adds wonderful, lacy texture to an arrangement (and the bees like it very much, so I'm glad to have it in the garden).

Next, I cut my chosen stems as long as possible. This allows for flexibility when placing them in the bowl or vase. It is always nice to have extra-tall flowers for the back or sides of the arrangement.

I start to group the shapes in my hand as I move through the plants. It gives a sort of preview of how the stems will be set up in the vessel. Then it's time to build the arrangement; page 188 offers step-by-step instructions.

CREATING THE ARRANGEMENT

1. Any arrangement begins with a support system. I have an assortment of metal flower frogs in a range of sizes and materials; here, I used my widest and heaviest pincushion frog. As an alternative, I sometimes use flower branches in the bottom of the bowl to support flower stems. I try to keep the structure as simple as possible, as it makes it easier to adjust things as I go along.

2. I cut a number of purple hyacinth bean branches that included leaves, blooms, and pods from the garden fence. I set aside a few stems and put the rest into the frog. These served to support the dahlia stems but all but disappeared as the flowers were added. I made sure, though, that one or two vines meandered off to the side so that they weren't totally lost from view.

3. Next, I placed the dahlias with largest heads and thickest stems, as I wanted them to be the focal points and to anchor the other stems.

4. I filled in the arrangement with smaller flower heads, including zinnias and small ball dahlias, to balance the colors across the composition. The creamy orange-white dahlias brightened up the other colors and lightened the overall effect of the stronger orange shades in the arrangement.

5. I wove in more delicate stems (including goldenrod, yellow wax bell, aster, rose hip, and morning glory) as they worked colorwise with the rest and added welcome texture.

6. I added smaller bits and brought the goldenrod toward the front, for an overall sense of lushness. The goldenrod at the back provided height. The reserved hyacinth bean vines, along with extra flower heads, around the foot of the bowl extend the arrangement.

1

4

Ten Lessons in Arranging

Composing an arrangement isn't easy to teach—you learn best by doing.
Renowned twentieth-century British floral designer Constance Spry
advised, "Just be natural and gay and light-hearted and pretty and simple and
overflowing and general and baroque and austere and stylized and wild and
daring and conservative and learn and learn. Open your minds to every form
of beauty." I try to follow her example, and to be newly inspired by each
opportunity. My education in the art of flower arranging continues. Here are
ten guidelines that I consider whenever I choose to create an arrangement in
one (or more) of my pots.

1. KEEP IT SIMPLE

A single variety of flower, in
one color, makes a powerful
statement. When the blossom
is exquisite, a vase filled with
nothing else allows you to enjoy
and contemplate its form and
texture. Play with the height
of the stems, allowing some to
stand tall and others to lean
over the rim of the vessel. I
cut the chrysanthemum stems
(pictured at left) extra long for
the tall vase I had in mind. This
lush, romantic variety, known
as 'Seaton's J'Dore', boasts
petals whose colors shift from
pink on the outer edge to yellow
at the center. Mums are often
used as supporting players
in mixed bouquets, but here
they take a well-deserved star
turn. Opposite, a footed bowl
is filled with my favorite roses,
'Constance Spry'. This old rose
blossoms only once a year,
so I wanted it to have its own
dedicated arrangement.

2. PLAY WITH PALETTE

Limiting yourself to flowers in a similar palette allows you to arrange something cohesive, with a focus on texture and composition. Some of the most impactful bouquets are those that feature one color scheme with subtle variations and abundant shapes and sizes, like the poppies, tulips, roses, and carnations shown opposite in a range of yellows (from soft and buttery to sunny and golden to bright and citrusy). They create a nice rhythm, mimicking the organic variations and contours in the ash-glazed porcelain vases. The lush, height-of-summer dahlias in the white tulipiere above are arranged in an ombré pattern, one of the easiest and most effective ways to display a bunch of blossoms in a similar palette.

3. BE BOLD

When you have brightly colored flowers, let their exuberance guide you. The deep fuchsia of the zinnias here complemented the boldness of the red and yellow ball dahlias. Nasturtiums provide an accent, with scarlet blooms and large, blue-green leaves. Opposite, I gathered poppies, hyacinth, tulips, anemones, daffodils, and clematis. I left the stems long so that the flowers explode out of the vase, with plenty of air in between. I also chose varieties with strong stems, to support the dramatic height of the flower heads.

4. BRANCH OUT FROM FLOWERS

Experimenting with non-floral subjects offers another lesson in composition. Here, I placed some late-fall crab apple cuttings in a classically shaped porcelain pot with an exaggerated pedestal, then filled a similarly footed bowl with misshapen apples on the cusp of decay. The colors are harmonious, but the shapes of the branches and fruit stand in marked contrast to each other, lending the display a wonderful sense of give-and-take.

5. FEATURE FOLIAGE

Leaves and vines can do much more than simply fill up space in an arrangement. In the sprawling still life, opposite, grape and raspberry vines weave in and around a footed bowl overrun with dahlias, cherry tomato stems, pomegranates, and figs. I composed the arrangement to celebrate the natural opulence of autumn, so the vines were given as much prominence as the flowers. By contrast, the "singular sensation" arrangement at right was born when I came upon a giant rhubarb leaf in the garden. Its size and shape were so magnificent that I immediately brought the leaf inside and set it into a pot, to show it off in all its glory.

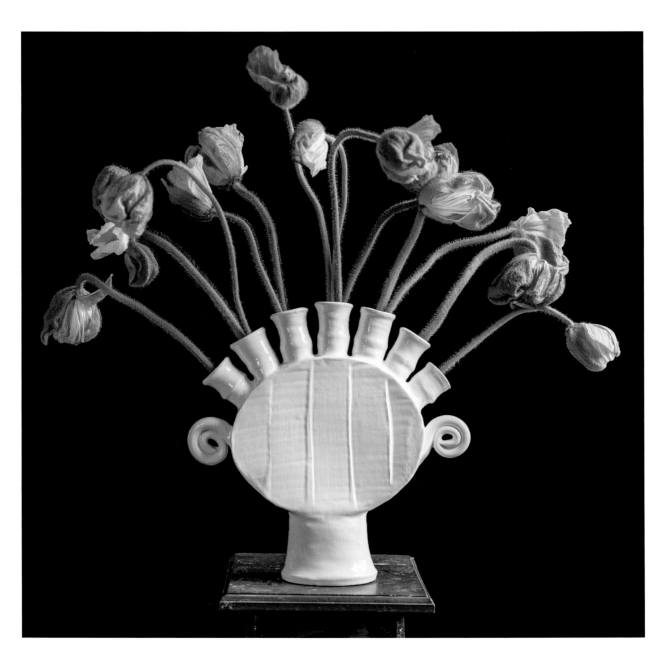

6. EMBRACE ALL
THEIR PHASES

A closed bud beginning to bloom is as powerful as a fully opened flower, and its subsequent waning can likewise transform the mood of an arrangement. Icelandic poppies (shown here), roses, peonies, and tulips are all excellent choices to showcase the span of budding, blooming, and fading. Not all flowers work in this way, however; a dahlia, for instance, will not change once it is cut, so I let mine remain in the garden until they have opened completely.

7. GIVE THEM SOME SUPPORT

All arrangements require reinforcement. I have a collection of flower frogs that I use to support my stems, as I prefer not to use flower foam or anything artificial for this task. Branches cut very short and placed in the vase or bowl can also provide an excellent foundation for flowers arranged in widemouthed vessels. Regardless of the method, it is best to organize the structure first before designing the composition. Pictured here are two possibilities for displaying my beloved bearded iris. The low bowl opposite is outfitted with a pin cushion–style flower frog, allowing me to show both stems and blooms (I don't mind that the support is visible). At right, one perfect iris stem is held in place by the narrow neck of the vase.

8. PUT THE VESSEL AND THE FLOWERS IN CONVERSATION

The relationship of the vessel to its contents is an essential consideration in arranging. When there is something blooming that needs to be celebrated, I decide which pot will best feature it. Other times, a new pot suggests what I should search for in the garden. The lesson here is to think of the flowers and vessel as collaborators, deep in conversation. At right, the black-red parrot tulips mimic the color and erratic form of the ash-glazed pot and its oxblood drips; it's almost as if the two were crying out to be paired together. The pyramid vases opposite were designed for tulips, but they work just as well for any long- and sturdy-stemmed flowers such as lilies or, as shown here, the last of the blowsy peonies that I needed to cut before an oncoming rainstorm flattened them.

9. THINK IN MULTIPLES

Reconsider the notion that an arrangement has to be one bunch in one vase. Try setting individual stems apart instead, for a relaxed but purposeful look. It's quicker, too, since you won't spend time fussing with stem placement. Choose small vessels that complement one another in some way (by palette, say, or shape). At left, I placed a vibrant assortment of tulips one by one in a series of glazed bud vases. With blooms veering off in different directions, the effect is jaunty rather than jumbled. Opposite, a group of ball dahlias were set in terra-cotta vases— but not in all of them. The use of negative space gives the eye an opportunity to see the pot forms as well as the flower shapes, and helps bring a sense of air and lightness.

10. MIND THE
SETTING AND SCALE

Consider the intended setting when determining the scale of your arrangement. I have vases that work well on a dinner table, where I want the flowers to be low enough that the guests can see one another and converse freely. At other times, a huge, extravagant vessel that will sit on an entry table allows me room to arrange with full abandon. In the photo opposite, the dahlias were at their most prolific, and I wanted to show off the magnificent dinner plate varieties. I included other flowers from the garden: amaranth, black hyacinth bean, nicotiana, and salvia. Above, one enormous 'Hamari Gold' dahlia begged to be showcased on its own. Any single-flower arrangement like this is lovely on a bedside table.

Documenting My Work

When I first met Wally, he taught me to use his Nikon F3 SLR camera. We brought it with us everywhere. A few years later, I began using it to document my first pieces of pottery. Through trial and error, I learned how to hang a roll of seamless paper, place the camera on a tripod, and record each pot before it left the studio. The early photos are not the clearest, but they are a visual documentation of what was made and sold then.

I have had long conversations with my photographer friend Marion Brenner about the technical aspects of the camera, and photography in general, including composition, exposure, and depth of field. In recent years, I have also worked with David Wagner, a photographer and Lightroom instructor, to learn more about photo processing and camera mechanics. Ultimately, however, it is the daily practice of taking photographs that has developed my visual vocabulary.

Once I've made my morning arrangement, I select the best spot in the studio to photograph it. I consider the overall color of the shot and how I wish to present the tableau. An east-facing window on the second floor with a black velvet backdrop is perfect for capturing the light just before the sun peeks over the trees. I start clicking the shutter, adjusting the aperture and speed as the light grows stronger. Unless it's cloudy, I avoid using the camera at midday, when the light is too bright and the contrast too harsh.

I have a series of tables and a collection of painted canvas backdrops to choose from. I prefer Farrow & Ball colors, for their great range and tremendous nuance. They react beautifully with light. A few of my favorite backdrop colors are Vardo (shown opposite), Dorset Cream, and Blue Ground.

I'll veer toward a richer color if the flowers are light. If the flowers are dark, I try to place a light-colored one toward the center for the lens to focus on; however, I move the point of focus around to cover all possibilities.

I use the raw mode for developing images in Lightroom. I try to avoid much tweaking, sometimes simply taking a flower or two out of shadow. My goal is to leave the photo as captured. I usually hold the camera with enough distance to allow for cropping the photo later on. Generally, I'm happiest with a 4-by-5-inch (10-by-13 cm) crop.

With just a few basic supplies, I've rigged up a system for photography in a corner of the studio. It consists of two tripods and one metal bar, with spring clamps to hold the canvas. I usually crop out the equipment, but sometimes I leave it in to give a "behind the scenes" context to the image.

Expanding Horizons

For many years, I photographed my work primarily for documentation and promotion purposes. I enclosed the photos in early publicity and marketing campaigns, with handwritten pitch letters to editors and retailers. Later, when I launched my website, the photographs became my most important sales tool. More recently, the audience for my photography has grown to include people I have met by way of social media.

I put my first website online in 2003. Up until 2010, customers would email me about pots that they wished to purchase, and sales were transacted via email, in person, and by mail with checks. I decided that year to make it easier for clients to purchase the work from the website.

Creating a digital presence has been an ongoing exercise. My website isn't the most sophisticated affair as these things go, but it gets the job done. It initially began with a simple graphic and gradually developed over time. I work with two wonderful designers who help me with the page designs and website mechanics. When I am busy and can't attend to the site, it has to fend for itself.

The website has required investment over a long period of time, and I have changed its mechanics as new technology became available. I need to keep abreast of style changes and simple tools, such as the search option and optimizing the website for mobile phone accessibility. Around 2010, I invested in online advertising to bring traffic to the site, mostly on wedding blogs, but I found that this was not worth the time or resources. It seems that the most critical aspect for the website and my work is to feature the best possible photographs, as this gives the most information for possible purchase or for editors sourcing product for articles.

Given the relationship between my photographs and the promotion of my work, it's natural that social media has had a large impact on the marketing of my business. I show the pots that are most interesting to me, along with flowers that are blooming in the garden, and hope this gives the viewer a sense of where I am heading creatively. It's easy to disparage the effect that social media has had on our culture, but it has introduced thousands of new followers to my business and led to several rewarding friendships and collaborations. I avoid using my account to share personal images, focusing instead on business strategy. I can tell, for example, which images garner an especially positive response, and I evaluate that information as I move forward. I try hard not to let social media monopolize my time and to limit my engagement to the early morning, while I'm having coffee and planning the day ahead. Then I usually post that morning's still-life photo, or announce an upcoming sale or other news, and head straight back to my seat at the wheel.

I've been honored to invite editors and clients whom I have met through social media to my studio. Many collaborative projects have begun at this table; last spring, my friends Anne Hardy and Imogen Pritchard, design manager of Plain English in New York City, joined me to plan a tea party at the Plain English showroom.

My Education in Photography

Though I constantly look at photography, there are a few artists I return to again and again. I often think of the paintings and etchings of Giorgio Morandi when I'm composing photographs, carefully debating the background, table, and object of each still life. Morandi had a small collection of objects that he repeatedly painted and placed on a table in his studio. Sometimes he composed groups of his props; in other paintings, he placed one by itself, making a single portrait. He was not concerned with the setting of a room or landscape, focusing instead on the dialogue between the object and the flat canvas. (The props and painting setups remain in Morandi's house in Bologna, which is now a museum. They were documented by Joel Meyerowitz in one of my favorite photography books, *Morandi's Objects*.)

I, too, prefer a more abstract environment for my work as opposed to a traditional room setting. I don't want the distraction of other elements in the photo. Sometimes, though, it is good to have a bit of context to break up the monotony of vases and flowers on a background, so I do environment shots from time to time.

Irving Penn's masterful compositions inspire me. His choices of tone, color, and subject matter are fascinating. I study his still lifes, of course, but I'm just as intrigued by his portraiture and fashion work for *Vogue*. I admire the simplicity, elegance, and sophistication in every one of Penn's photographs, and they prompt me to consider how I style my pots as bodies in the frame. The takeaway from his work, for me, is learning to recognize when it's time to stand back and let a subject speak for itself.

I study Constantin Brâncuşi's black-and-white photos of his studio to see his sculptures as he wished them to be understood. Brâncuşi felt that other photographers did not capture the essence of his work, so he asked Edward Steichen to teach him how to use the camera in order to document the studio himself. I learned to photograph because I felt that no one would see the pots as I do.

In homage to Morandi, I assemble pots in groups—often five, but always an odd number—to play with the forms and document their relationships. Clockwise from top left: a freshly unloaded collection of ash glazes, various celadons, vases from my first wood firing, and a comparison of porcelain bisque to earthenware.

Four Photographic Principles

I keep my photography process fairly minimal, preferring straightforward images, each with a clear story to tell. First, I determine the purpose of the photo. Is it meant to be an artful still life, a documentation of my work or my flowers, or something in between? Either way, I shoot in natural rather than artificial light because I prefer the resulting photographs, as well as the convenience of using what's available as opposed to bringing in additional equipment. I keep the following principles in mind as I shoot.

1. LIGHT

Early and late light each produce a different feeling; my vision for a given image determines the location in which I shoot. In the morning, there is a brief moment when the day brightens through an east-facing window on the second floor of the studio. I wait at this spot so as not to miss the chance to exploit the dramatic contrast of light and shadow. The photo of persimmons in a footed, shino-glazed bowl opposite was captured at the break of dawn. At the end of the day (the so-called golden hour), as the sun drops behind the trees, the light at the west-facing window on the first floor of the studio is quite even, resulting in flatter, more peaceful compositions. The moment is not as fleeting, so I'm able to use a tripod to shoot, as I did with the spider chrysanthemums in the terra-cotta vase shown at left. (I avoid taking photographs in the middle of the day because of harsh shadows.)

2. CONTRAST

Just as light is key to the emotion of the photograph, contrast influences its sensibility. Here is a pot with tulips, cherry branches, and narcissi, shot against both a favorite chartreuse backdrop and a black velvet one. The flowers set against the black backdrop appear brighter, their outlines more accentuated; this composition references the dark surroundings of a classic Dutch still life. The eye goes to the individual red, pink, and white flowers, and the pot becomes less important. The same arrangement shown on the oval table against the lighter background is much softer and evokes a tranquil, dreamy feeling, especially as the back edge of the table blurs into the background. The neutral green and taupe create an overall composition that is more contemplative and serene.

3. WARM VERSUS COOL

When planning a photograph, I think in terms of the overall color temperature and mood I wish to project. If I want something warm and lush, I gravitate to reds and oranges. For the photo opposite, I chose the red plane of the table and a red backdrop to blend in with the arrangement and its pops of warmth from the red amaryllis, orange tulips, and bright pink hyacinths. The red pomegranates and persimmons in the foreground further emphasize the lushness. In comparison, the blue hyacinths shown above were photographed in early March, at the end of their bloom. I wanted the overripe blossoms to have a cold, mysterious feeling, so I placed them on the black table in front of the black curtain and kept the light quite low and the blue color, strong. The black surroundings intensified the shadows of the hyacinth flowers and kept everything in that same coolness of tone.

4. POINT OF VIEW

Some days, I wish to contemplate or document one flower; at other times, I choose to photograph an abundant still life displaying the day's garden bounty. Point of view helps tell the story. The perspective can be either straight ahead, in the manner of portraiture, or from above, the better to see the faces of the flowers. I consider the photo above a portrait of deep summer, with its abundance of zinnias, peaches, and tomatoes; I included the watermelon, which I did not grow, as an homage to my hero Irving Penn, the master of the still life portrait. The colors are of equal intensity. For the photo opposite, I chose to shoot armloads of dahlias on the tennis court from overhead. I had just picked them, and I wanted to make a record of the gorgeous variety of shapes and patterns that can't be seen as easily in a full bouquet. It also serves as a reference in the winter, when I try to remember which flowers I planted in a particular year.

ON THE INNER VOICE

The same inner voice that guides my business decisions carries over into the physical process in my studio. At times I have put raw or unfinished pots on the floor even after telling myself, "Do not put that pot on the floor, because surely you will step on it." Then the other side of this imaginary conversation counters, "Oh, no, I will see it and step around it," so I leave it there. Later on, when I am not thinking, I inevitably knock it over and the piece is ruined. Why did I not move it after telling myself to? I knew this would happen, as it has over and over through the years. I acknowledge the loss, then throw the raw piece into the forsythia bushes outside my studio or put the fired pot in the garbage. I move on, hoping that I will not do such stupid things in the future. And yet, I do.

Last summer I was very excited about a footed bowl I had made. The pedestal was long and slim, and I had a vision of photographing it with a tall column of dahlias. I danced around the kiln waiting for the pots to cool down, then immediately pulled out the bowl and placed it on the table. I constructed a tower of raw clay for anchoring the stems, then picked a beautiful group of dinner-plate dahlias. As I was placing the stems in the wet clay, I saw that the mound was unstable, but I kept going anyway.

After I took the photograph, I was eager to process it on the computer. As I left the studio, the column was slowly shifting forward from the weight of the dahlias. I said to myself, "Take those flowers out of the bowl before leaving," but I ignored this admonition and ran into the house to process the shot in Lightroom on my computer.

About twenty minutes later, I remembered the precarious arrangement and returned to the studio. The table was empty, without bowl or flowers. I looked on the floor: Sure enough, there was my new bowl broken in half with my column of dahlias splattered on the floor. I actually started to laugh, as I had known this would happen. Once again, why didn't I listen to myself? Now after photographing a flower arrangement, I am careful to move the vase off the table and onto the floor so that there is no way for it to fall.

Occasionally, I meet a prospective client who I immediately know will be challenging. I caution myself, "Do not accept this commission; it will not be worth it." It took years, but I have finally learned to turn down jobs based on this intuition. It is immensely liberating to learn how to say no. This creates a truer work environment, because I am committed to making work that brings joy. And the clay senses my goodwill, which is imbued in the pot and is critical to the outcome.

ALMOND CAKE

This recipe is a reminder of a time when listening to the voice in my head worked out especially well. One evening at my sister-in-law Pamela's home in San Francisco, this cake was served for dessert. It was so delicious that I had to learn how to make it myself. I was determined to get the recipe right then and there. I followed the chef, who was also Pam's secretary, around the house until she printed out the recipe for me. It was a good thing, too, as she left the job the next day. I have, in turn, given this recipe to nearly every person I know. It is a no-fail cake for parties, and it is absolutely divine. *Makes one 8-inch (20 cm) cake; serves 8*

8 tablespoons (1 stick/113 g) unsalted
   butter, plus more for the pan
¼ cup (30 g) all-purpose flour, plus more for
   the pan
7 ounces (200 g) almond paste
   (I use Odense brand)

¾ cup (150 g) granulated sugar
3 large eggs, lightly beaten
¼ teaspoon almond extract
2 tablespoons (30 ml) Grand Marnier
½ teaspoon baking powder
Confectioner's sugar, for dusting

Preheat the oven to 350°F (180°C). Butter and flour an 8-inch (20 cm) round cake pan.

Break up the almond paste and place it in the bowl of a food processor with the sugar. Pulse until the mixture is granular, 30 seconds to 1 minute. Cut the butter into tablespoons. Add it to the bowl and pulse until the ingredients are creamy and blended. Add the eggs, almond extract, and Grand Marnier and pulse until blended. Whisk to combine the flour and baking powder; add to the bowl and pulse a few times to combine.

Transfer the batter to the prepared pan. Bake until a cake tester comes out cleanly, about 35 minutes. Transfer the pan to a wire rack to cool for 10 to 15 minutes before inverting the cake onto the rack to cool completely. The cake will be quite soft and dense. It can be kept in an airtight container at room temperature up to 1 day ahead. Dust with confectioner's sugar just before serving.

Forcing Bulbs in Pots

When the garden is dormant and I don't have new flowers to cut and arrange for photographs, I like to force bulbs in my terra-cotta pots. This takes a little bit of forethought, as ideally the bulbs should be planted in October, then placed in either a cold frame outside or in a cold basement. It is exciting to see the shoots emerge from the soil and to feel that spring is not far behind. I stick to one type of flower per pot, but some growers advocate layering different types one over the other, such as tulip on the bottom, then narcissus, and finally muscari.

To begin, select a pot with a drainage hole, large enough to accommodate the size of the bulb and subsequent bloom. If you are unsure what size pot is required, ask the bulb supplier to recommend the diameter. At the bottom of the pot, place a layer of small pebbles—the kind that might go on a garden path, sold at any garden supply center. Then add a few inches (5 cm) of organic potting soil over the pebbles. Place the bulbs very close together in the pot, as it looks odd to have flowers widely spaced once they sprout and begin to bloom. The planting depth will vary depending on the size of the bulb and its flower; there is usually an instruction manual included in the bulb order for reference. Fill in around the bulbs with potting soil. I cover the planted pots with plastic netting, as the mice or chipmunks that find their way into the barn basement during the cold

months love to dig in and eat the bulbs. It's a big disappointment when you look for a bulb to poke through in February, only to realize that it was eaten in November!

Put the pots somewhere cold. My barn basement never quite freezes, though it teeters on the edge. This seems acceptable for the twelve-week dormancy required for spring blooms, even if they are not planted in the garden. (I've read that pots can also go in the refrigerator, but I've not tried this approach, as my fridge is usually filled with groceries.)

Once the bulbs are planted, water them about every two weeks. It is important not to overwater, as the bulbs are supposed to be dormant, but if they were outside, they would be watered by rain and snow. Aim to keep them somewhat damp, until they are ready to be brought up into the warmth and sunlight. When you see the bulbs begin to sprout in spite of the cold, take them out of cold storage and place them by a window. It is cheering to watch them grow and take shape. The leaves alone are a welcome promise that spring will arrive.

Once the flowers have opened, I often cut them and place them in a vase. I let the bulbs dry out and plant them in the garden for the following year. There is no guarantee that they will bloom a second time, but I can't bear to simply compost them. Once again, hope springs eternal.

I keep a collection of terra-cotta pots in a range of sizes. Most have wide bowls, to accommodate multiple bulbs. The footed urn on page 230 holds nearly two dozen densely planted orange princess tulips. On page 231, a collection of pots filled with forced hyacinths (*H. orientalis* 'Pink Pearl'), muscari (*M. armeniacum* 'Valerie Finnis' and *aucheri* 'Blue Magic'), and narcissi (*N.* 'Sovereign') brings to mind a walk in the garden in early spring.

ON BEING KIND TO YOURSELF

A few years ago, I read Atul Gawande's book *Being Mortal*. His insistence that we take care of our bodies as we age, to keep them strong for later years, completely resonated with me. My whole adult life, a goal of mine has been to be fit, eat well, and basically follow the middle road on self-care—nothing too extreme in either direction. Now that I'm in my sixties, I make an effort to set aside enough time for physical activity and rest, with equal attention granted to both.

I try to take a barre class or go for a walk every day. It is easy to find reasons not to follow through with this plan, but if exercise is marked on the calendar, it is much harder to ignore. Exercising early in the day can also fend off the physical and mental energy slump that might otherwise hit around three o'clock in the afternoon.

Mental well-being is as vital as physical fitness. Simple measures such as stopping work when I am tired and scheduling breaks in the workday make profound differences in my psyche. I've been asked what I do when I find myself in a work slump, but in thirty years of business, I can't say that I've truly experienced one. Or at least I haven't found myself in such a funk that I can't lift myself out. The key is to nip a bad mood in the bud before it affects the work. The best way to do this is to step away from the studio.

When I feel any sort of ennui setting in, I try to assign it a value. Is this something that can be overcome with a quick fix, like a cup of tea or a walk in the garden? Or do I need to get to a stopping point in my work and plan an impromptu day in the city? Is it time to schedule a longer period of time away? Just knowing that I have something planned is a good way to keep me balanced and productive.

The main thing is to define what wellness means to you, and to make it as much a part of your routine as is required. You simply cannot succeed without it. When I am overwhelmed with various tasks and responsibilities, I call my children. They always say, "Be kind to yourself." This reminder puts stress into perspective. In those troubled moments, I do something else until I feel calm again.

MINESTRONE

One strategy to get me out of a work stalemate is to cook or bake. Simply walking from the studio into the kitchen changes my focus and restores my equilibrium. I visit the local farmers' market or farm stand to see what is fresh and available. For example, our neighbors—the wonderful, organic Ambler Farm—sell produce from a stand twice a week, starting in spring. This recipe includes all the vegetables I found at the farm one Saturday morning—they were all too beautiful to leave behind. But this is merely a guide; any substitutions will do. I include fregola, but you can omit it if you want the soup to be gluten-free. *Serves 8*

6 tablespoons (90 ml) olive oil

2 leeks, white and light green parts only, trimmed, washed well, and finely chopped

2 cups (230 g) peeled and diced butternut squash

2½ pounds (1.1 kg) diced potatoes

1½ cups (143 g) chopped string beans

2 cups (300 g) shelled fresh broad beans, such as cranberry or Romano

1 small knob celery root, peeled and chopped (about 1 cup/130 g)

2 carrots (medium to large), sliced

2 cups (270 g) cauliflower florets

2 cups (160 g) chopped eggplant

2 celery stalks, sliced

2 or 3 shiitake mushrooms, sliced

2 cups (130 g) shredded kale

2 plum tomatoes, chopped

1 teaspoon red pepper flakes

2 garlic cloves, minced

Coarse salt and freshly ground black pepper

⅓ cup (67 g) fregola (optional)

8 cups (2 l) chicken or vegetable stock or water

Chopped fresh parsley or cilantro, for garnish

Warm the olive oil in a large pot over medium-low heat. Add the leeks, squash, and potatoes and sauté, stirring occasionally, for 10 minutes, or until softened.

Add the string beans, broad beans, celery root, carrots, cauliflower, eggplant, celery, mushrooms, kale, tomatoes, red pepper flakes, and garlic. Season with salt and black pepper. Sauté for 10 minutes, stirring occasionally. Add the fregola, if using, and the stock. Bring it to a boil, then reduce the heat to low and simmer for about an hour, or until the vegetables are tender but not mushy. Season to taste with salt and black pepper, sprinkle with fresh herbs, and serve.

Always a Student

When I started making pots, producing white earthenware clay and painting it like a canvas was my foremost goal. As I mastered this technique, I felt I needed to learn how to throw and fire translucent porcelain. This required a more complex gas-fired kiln that achieved higher temperatures, then learning how to make glazes by following ceramic formulas. Most recently, I yearned for yet another firing option: a wood-fired kiln. I wanted to experiment with pottery that could be produced only in this type of environment. Though gas and wood kilns can achieve the same high temperatures, the results of the firings are very different. In the gas kiln, the reduction atmosphere creates opportunity for gorgeous glaze colors. In the wood environment, although there is a similar reduction atmosphere, the ash from the wood falls onto the pots and literally becomes part of the glaze. There is a much more random, elemental, and unpredictable aspect to the wood flame that enhances the beauty of the pots. In addition, there are stoneware and porcelain clays, as well as glazes, formulated especially for the wood-kiln flame. I also love that it is the oldest and most elemental approach to firing the work.

I was referred to Tyler Gulden, a potter in Maine, who designed a wood kiln specifically for me. I asked for a kiln that could be fired in one day by one person. He named this kiln "minigama," a smaller version of the anagama, a kiln that originated in China in the fifth century and is still used by potters worldwide in various iterations. Tyler arrived at my house one morning in May and spent the next five days building the kiln outside my studio.

My first firing in the new wood kiln was incredibly exciting—and involved much more work than I had envisioned.

Below: After pots are loaded, the wood kiln is closed up with two rows of bricks.

Opposite: Once the walls are deconstructed, I can see immediately how the ash and flame hit the pots in different areas of the kiln, informing the next firing.

It takes hours to strategically load the pots into the kiln and place bricks just so to guide the path of the flame throughout the kiln. Once the kiln was loaded and the front bricked up, the firing began. Recently, Wally and I did a second firing and discovered that loading the wood just as the kiln temperature crested from the burst of energy created by the previous stoke kept the overall temperature climbing. This happened every four to seven minutes, depending on the size and amount of logs placed in the pit. The firing cycle went on for about twelve hours, but the time seemed to go by quickly somehow.

It takes about six days before the kiln completely cools down and can be opened. Then the analysis can begin, and I learn a great deal. It will take time for me to master how to balance the flame disbursement so that the pots at the front of the kiln are not overfired and those at the back top are not underfired. Some glazes that were good for the gas kiln—such as the oxblood— were not necessarily good for the wood kiln. The ash and shino glazes seemed happiest in the wood-fired environment. There are infinite possibilities for experimentation, and of course all

of this could change once I learn to manage the flame. The tests and trials will go on, but ultimately I am thrilled to have realized a long-held dream.

Following pages: These pots, from my second wood firing, show the beauty and variety that results from the combination of clay bodies (porcelain or stoneware), glazes, and ash that rains on the pots as the kiln temperature climbs and the wood furiously burns.

ON LOOKING STRAIGHT AHEAD

Many years ago, I participated in the well-known and -attended annual gift show at the Javits Convention Center in New York City. I was completely daunted and overwhelmed. All the other booths looked bigger, better organized, and definitely more pulled together than mine. What was I thinking, with my tiny company, trying to compete with much more established vendors? When my friend David Hopkins, then the national manager for the Metropolitan Museum shops, came into my booth, I started to cry. He said, "Don't look right, don't look left; look straight ahead." With those simple words, he reminded me that I can only put my own best efforts forward, and that nothing good comes from comparing yourself with others.

I think of this line every time I'm challenged to maintain focus. It works for me on so many levels. One simply has to stick to one's vision and not get distracted by myriad things that exist in the world. Whenever my eye starts to go astray and the voice of self-doubt creeps in, I take a deep breath, recall David's advice, and get back on track.

This mantra also resonates with me as I seek to stretch my work in uncharted directions. In pottery (as in everything, frankly), trends come and go. It's easy to get bogged down, but I work hard to not pay attention to trends but rather stay true to myself in whatever I make.

I return always to the goal I began with thirty some years ago: to make functional and beautiful ceramics. Recently, I was asked to design a collection of pots for a trunk show at the home furnishings shop KRB in Manhattan. I know that the owner, Kate Brodsky, loves color, so I endeavored to introduce a vibrant element; I thought of slipware, developed in ancient China, that calls for using colored earthenware slip to apply decorative patterns to pottery. The result was a set of platters (pictured opposite) that felt new and yet still of a piece with my existing body of work. Kate and her customers were delighted with the platters. I plan to make more, and am eager to see in what direction they take me next.

Sources

BEARDED IRISES

Pleasants Valley Iris Farm
irisfarmer.com

Schreiner's Iris Gardens
schreinersgardens.com

BULBS

Brent and Becky's
brentandbeckysbulbs.com

K. van Bourgondien
dutchbulbs.com

Old House Gardens
oldhousegardens.com

Van Engelen Inc.
vanengelen.com

CHRYSANTHEMUMS

King's Mums
kingsmums.com

CLAY

Aardvark
aardvarkclay.com

Brackers
brackers.com

Ceramic Supply Inc.
ceramic-supply-inc.myshopify.com

Sheffield Pottery
sheffield-pottery.com

Standard Ceramic
standardceramic.com

DAHLIAS

Aztec Dahlias
aztecdahlias.com

Bear Creek Farm
bearcreekfarm.com

Brent and Becky's
brentandbeckysbulbs.com

DAHLIAaddict
dahliaaddict.com

Endless Summer Flower Farm
endlesssummerflowerfarm.com

Ferncliff Gardens
ferncliffgardens.com

Old House Gardens
oldhousegardens.com

Swan Island Dahlias
dahlias.com

FLOWER AND GARDEN TOOLS

Felco
felco.com

Floral Genius
floralgenius.com

Jamali Garden
jamaligarden.com

Womanswork
womanswork.com

PEONIES

Adelman Peony Gardens
peonyparadise.com

Peony's Envy
peonysenvy.com

ROSES

The Antique Rose Emporium
antiqueroseemporium.com

David Austin Roses
davidaustinroses.com

SEEDS, HERBS, AND PLANTS

Annie's Annuals & Perennials
anniesannuals.com

Floret
floretflowers.com

Gilbertie's Organics
gilbertiesorganics.com

Johnny's Selected Seeds
johnnyseeds.com

Renee's Garden
reneesgarden.com

Row 7 Seed Company
row7seeds.com

Select Seeds
selectseeds.com

Snug Harbor Farm
snugharborfarm.com

Further Reading

A note: Some of books listed below are old and out of print and may be easiest to locate in a library. I have tried to largely include books that are readily available, but some of the rarer ones are too important to my work to omit.

CERAMICS

Ash Glazes by Phil Rogers
A reference for ash glaze recipes, including explanations of approaches by different artists as well as glaze technology.

The Beauty of Everyday Things by Sōetsu Yanagi
Essays on Japanese aesthetics.

Bernard Leach by Edmund de Waal
A biography of the pivotal English potter who brought Shōji Hamada to the United Kingdom and the world at large and started the Leach Pottery in St. Ives, Cornwall.

Centering in Pottery, Poetry, and the Person by M. C. Richards
An exploration of the process of making ceramics as it connects to poetry and meditation.

Colour in Glazes and *Science for Potters* by Linda Bloomfield
Two books focusing on glaze chemistry and formulation.

The Complete Guide to High-Fire Glazes by John Britt
An explanation of glaze chemistry.

Creation out of Clay: The Ceramic Art and Writings of Brother Thomas, edited by Rosemary Williams
A catalog of Brother Thomas's work and inventive use of form and glaze.

Hamada Potter by Bernard Leach
A discussion with master potter Shōji Hamada exploring his aesthetics of craft pottery.

Lucie Rie by Tony Birks
A biography of the illustrious potter as well as a catalog of her exquisite work.

The Mad Potter of Biloxi: The Art and Life of George E. Ohr by Garth Clark
An essential biography of the brilliant potter from Biloxi, Mississippi, who threw extraordinary earthenware.

The Potter's Book of Glaze Recipes and *Ten Thousand Years of Pottery* by Emmanuel Cooper
Two important tomes from an expert on glazes and ceramics history.

The Potter's Complete Book of Clay and Glazes by James Chappell
A compendium of glaze recipes.

Things of Beauty Growing: British Studio Pottery edited by Glenn Adamson
The catalog of the Yale Center for British Art 2017 exhibition that showed British studio pottery from the early twentieth century to the present.

The Unknown Craftsman: A Japanese Insight into Beauty by Sōetsu Yanagi; adapted by Bernard Leach
A discussion of Japanese craft and usefulness.

Warren Mackenzie: An American Potter by David Lewis
A biography of this master potter, with photos and glaze recipes.

The White Road: Journey into an Obsession by Edmund de Waal
A fascinating history of porcelain and its development over the globe.

COOKING

Bradley Ogden's Breakfast, Lunch, and Dinner
by Bradley Ogden
A fantastic cookbook written in 1991, at the forefront of new California cooking.

Canal House: Cook Something by Christopher Hirsheimer and Melissa Hamilton
The latest and incredibly useful contribution by the authors of numerous cookbooks.

Cannelle et Vanille: Nourishing Gluten-Free Recipes for Every Meal and Mood by Aran Goyoaga
A modern and gluten-free approach to classic delicious recipes.

Chez Panisse Café Cookbook by Alice Waters and the cooks at Chez Panisse
My first and favorite volume by Waters—it's timeless.

Happiness Is Baking by Maida Heatter
Just one of the many cookbooks worthy of collecting from this ultimate old-school baker.

The James Beard Cookbook by James Beard
A classic American cookbook.

Martha Stewart's Pies and Tarts by Martha Stewart
The cookbook, among Stewart's many excellent offerings, always on rotation in my kitchen.

Salt, Fat, Acid, Heat: Mastering the Elements of Good Cooking by Samin Nosrat
An essential volume on cooking theory.

The Silver Palate Cookbook by Sheila Lukins and Julee Rosso
A required classic for any kitchen library; my well-thumbed original copy has basically fallen apart.

Tartine: A Classic Revisited by Elisabeth Prueitt and Chad Robertson
A contemporary approach to baking and bread making that incorporates many heirloom grains.

GARDENING

The Brother Gardeners: A Generation of Gentlemen Naturalists and the Birth of an Obsession by Andrea Wulf
An excellent examination of seven eighteenth-century botanists who formed the foundations of contemporary garden design.

The Cutting Garden: Growing and Arranging Garden Flowers by Sarah Raven
An enviable array of flowers and how to grow them (in the United Kingdom).

Floret Farm's A Year in Flowers by Erin Benzakein
An expert flower growing and arranging manual.

Flower Decoration by Constance Spry
The first book by the original rock-star florist, who conceived a whole new approach to composing arrangements beginning in the 1920s and continuing into the 1950s.

A Gentle Plea for Chaos by Mirabel Osler
A look at one woman's garden and how she encouraged its design to be unstructured and spontaneous.

The Land Gardeners: Cut Flowers by Bridget Elworthy and Henrietta Courtauld
A beautiful guide to flower growing and soil health as well as a showcase for Elworthy and Courtauld's garden.

Martha's Flowers by Martha Stewart and Kevin Sharkey
A guide to exquisite flower arrangements and how to choose blooms to grow for bouquets.

On Flowers by Amy Merrick
Merrick's original views on flower arranging, travel, and how to live with beauty.

Planting with Colour: The Transformation of Hadspen Garden by Nori and Sandra Pope
A wonderful resource from a bygone garden (the property is now a hotel). Flower photos are arranged by color—my favorite way to choose what to plant.

Scent Magic: Notes from a Gardener by Isabel Bannerman
A well-researched and informative examination of the garden through the lens of scent.

Some Flowers by Vita Sackville-West
A 1937 celebration of twenty-five of her favorite flowers by Sackville-West, famed for her brilliantly designed Sissinghurst Garden in England.

Spirit: Garden Inspiration by Dan Pearson
The important contemporary garden designer discusses places and gardens that have influenced his thinking.

A Way to Garden by Margaret Roach
A twentieth-anniversary, revised edition of an excellent all-around guide to planting a garden; one of my first gardening books and still completely relevant.

The Well-Tempered Garden by Christopher Lloyd
The epic British gardener discusses his own garden, Great Dixter, and teaches how to experiment with plants.

A Year in Flowers by Shane Connolly
A tome from the au courant British designer responsible for a whole new aesthetic of foraging and arranging flowers.

PHOTOGRAPHY

Brâncuşi: The Photographs by Constantin Brâncuşi
A catalog of photographs that Brâncuşi took of his sculpture, flower still lifes, and other subjects connected to his work.

Camera Work: A Critical Anthology, edited by Jonathan Green
A catalog of the photography journal from around 1903, showcasing avant-garde photographers from that era.

Dorothea Lange: Words & Pictures by Sarah Meister
A collection of essays accompanying the recent MoMA retrospective discussing the importance and timelessness of Lange's photography.

Irving Penn: Centennial by Irving Penn
A posthumous tome that includes the majority of the photographic work Penn produced in his long career.

Looking at Photographs: 100 Pictures from the Collection of the Museum of Modern Art by John Szarkowski
The iconic book, originally published in 1973, that looks at photographers and explains what makes a brilliant composition.

Morandi's Objects by Joel Meyerowitz
An artful documentation of the familiar objects from Morandi's paintings, found in the Italian's studio (now a museum).

The Photographer in the Garden by Jamie M. Allen and Sarah Anne McNear
A collection from the Eastman Museum exploring the history of garden photography.

Why People Photograph by Robert Adams
A classic text on looking at photographs, with essays on various artists and photography considerations.

Acknowledgments

Writing and taking the photographs for this book has been a splendid journey, and there are many people to acknowledge for helping me bring it to completion.

I would like to thank Carla Glasser, my literary agent and friend, who urged me to write. She has been my champion every step of the way. I am truly grateful.

Ellen Morrissey has been my collaborator on this project since its inception. Her editorial experience and intelligence, as well as her aesthetic sensibilities, have shaped these pages. I thank her for her time and patience.

Thank you to publisher Lia Ronnen for encouraging and understanding my vision as well as supporting the hard work necessary to make the book come to life.

Thank you to my editor at Artisan, Bridget Monroe Itkin, whose graciousness and professionalism have been a gift. Her knowledge and point of view have been essential to the book's development and outcome.

Thank you to Elizabeth Van Itallie for her graceful book design. She has presented my words and images marvelously. And thank you to Jane Treuhaft for her keen eye and expertise with the imagery, layouts, and production.

Thank you to all those at Artisan involved in making and promoting this book: Sibylle Kazeroid, Paula Brisco, Suet Chong, Nancy Murray, Elise Ramsbottom, Bella Lemos, Allison McGeehon, Theresa Collier, Amy Michelson, and Patrick Thedinga.

Thank you to Dominique Browning for her thoughtful and beautifully written foreword. Our friendship has been a wonderful exchange over these many years.

Thank you to Marion Brenner, who taught me how to understand the camera and bring my imagined photos into reality. And thank you for my portrait—I remember that day!

Thank you to Jane Beiles for my author portrait.

Thank you also to David Wagner for his technical expertise, which has educated me enormously.

Thank you to Kim Risolo, my bookkeeper and sounding board in my business for over a decade. I appreciate her daily help, and our friendship.

And thank you to Connie (Consuelo Quesada), who has helped me organize my life in and out of the studio for over thirty years.

Thank you to Johanna Pfund, whom I have worked with since the launch of my website, and who is responsible for its bones. And to Kate Caprari, for her elegant design of my website and promotional materials.

Thank you to Pamela and C. Richard Kramlich, my sister- and brother-in-law, who have been my crusaders since we met at the Odeon Restaurant in 1985! I value their eternal enthusiasm and love them very much.

I am grateful to my many friends who have inspired and supported my work. Writing this book, I've been especially indebted to a few for their guidance, namely, Barbara Callahan, Phoebe Cole-Smith, Leslie Giuliani, Anne Hardy, Pauline Kelley, and Zizi Mueller.

Thank you to Laurie Glatzer of BodyQuest barre studio in Westport, Connecticut, whose classes help me stay mentally and physically balanced.

Thank you to all of my clients, who are also friends, and have inspired my work since the beginning.

Thank you to all the editors, writers and photographers whom I have worked with over the years.

Thank you to the retailers who have supported my work these last three decades: Aerin Lauder at Aerin, Paulette and John Peden and Jane Fredrikson at Dawn Hill Antiques, Jenah Barry at Fotografiska New York, Suzanne Rheinstein at Hollyhock, Kate Brodsky and Ani Kaplowitz at KRB NYC, Lauren

Santo Domingo at Moda Operandi, Renée Price and Paul Landy at Neue Galerie, David Hopkins and David Wilson at North Haven Gallery, Bunny Williams at 100 Main, Ben Pentreath and Bridie Hall at Pentreath & Hall, Tony Elliott and Stephanie Pilk at Snug Harbor Farm, the team at Terrain, and Wave Hill.

Thank you to Grace Kennedy for your help with the garden. To East Coast Wholesale Flowers, the flower company that gets me through the winter months when my garden is sleeping. To Andre Carvalho, who has helped me keep the property together. And to Laura Mulligan, who is always up for any flower project.

Thank you to Larry Liggett, who is always on board to design something special for the garden or wood kiln. Thank you to Peter Hansen, for your ongoing help with flowers, pots, and all Kramlich concerns in California.

And finally, thank you to Wally, Daphne, David, Cooper, Martina, and Ethan. I love them more than these words could ever convey.

Index

Page numbers in *italics* refer to photo captions.

A

Alice's Adventures in Wonderland and Through the Looking-Glass (Carroll), 50
almond cake, 226
Ambler Farm, 235
American Dahlia Society, 135
Anna Karenina (Tolstoy), 45
apple tarte tatin, 98
Armstrong, Louis, 97
art, 23, 25
art books, 166
ash glazes, 69, *74*

B

baking and cooking, 166, 235
  see also recipes
Barry, Jenah, *183*
Beauty of Everyday Things, The (Sōetsu), 13, 19
bees, *134, 186*
  beekeeping, 161, *161, 163*
being kind to yourself, 232
Being Mortal (Gawande), 232
Bell, Vanessa, 50, 140
Benzakein, Erin, 186
Bezanson, Brother Thomas, 66
bisque firing, 38, *42,* 50
Bleak House (Dickens), 177
Bone Simple, *183*
books, 166, *166*
  audiobooks, 177
Brâncuşi, Constantin, 46, 214
bread, date-nut, 169

Brenner, Marion, 152, 210
Brodsky, Kate, 241
Browning, Dominique, 10–13, *10, 152*
bulbs, forcing in pots, 229, *229*
business promotion, 34–35
Bute, Lady, 134

C

cake, almond, 226
cake plates, 50, *52*
Carroll, Lewis, 50
Cavanilles, Antonio José, 134
celadon glaze, 66, 69, *72, 87*
centering, 32
Centering in Pottery, Poetry, and the Person (Richards), 32
ceramics, *see* pottery and ceramics
Cetti, Livia, 183
cheese and leek tart, 30
Chez Panisse Menu Cookbook (Waters), 30
chicken, perfect roast, 174
Child, Julia, 98
children, 105, 170
Chinese pottery, 46–49, 64, 67, 69, *97,* 241
chrysanthemums, *190, 216*
cobalt painting, *38,* 64, *64*
Cole-Smith, Phoebe, 19
collaboration, 64, 183
cookbooks, 166
cooking and baking, 166, 235
  see also recipes
Cycladic pottery, *23,* 46, 54, *78, 88*

D

Dahl, Andreas, 134
dahlias, 124–35, *124, 134,* 143, *152, 183, 193, 206, 209, 223*
  examples of, 135, *136–39*
  how to grow, 126–31
date-nut bread, 169
deadlines, 177
Dickens, Charles, 177
documenting work, 179, 210, *210,* 213, 214, *214,* 216

E

earthenware, *25,* 37, 38, 50–54, *50, 52, 58,* 241
Edgarton, Harold, *82*
1882 Ltd., 183, *183*
Etruscan pottery, *46,* 54, 78
exercise, 110, 232

F

Floret Flowers, 186
flower arranging, step-by-step, 186–88
flower arranging, ten lessons in, 190
  boldness, *194*
  color palette, *193*
  foliage, *199*
  multiples, *206*
  non-floral subjects, *196*
  phases of flowers, *200*
  relationship of flowers to vessel, *205*
  setting and scale, *209*
  simplicity, *190*
  support, *203*
flower molds, 156, *158*

flowers
  chrysanthemums, *190, 216*
  dahlias, *see* dahlias
  forcing bulbs in pots, 229, *229*
  irises, *140, 148, 203*
  muscari, *147, 229*
  narcissi, *144, 229*
  peonies, *148, 200, 205*
  poppies, *147, 193, 194, 200*
  roses, *190, 193, 200*
  tulips, *144, 193, 194, 200, 205,*
    206, 229
  see also garden
focus, 241
Fotografiska New York, 35, *183*
Franklin, Benjamin, 45
friends, 173

G

garden, 120, *120,* 186
  happy accidents in, 152
  inspirations for, 140
  planting strategy for, 143, *143*
  spring blooms in, 144, *144, 147,*
    148
Garden Conservancy, 140
gardening books, 166
garden pots, 50, 55
Gawande, Atul, 232
Giacometti, Alberto, 46
glazes, 38, 66–67, *66*
  ash, 69, *74*
  celadon, 66, 69, *72, 87*
  oribe, 67, *73*
  oxblood, 66, 67–69, *70, 74*
  shino, *68,* 69
goat cheese and leek tart, 30
Grant, Duncan, 50, 140

grape hyacinth (muscari), *147, 229*
Green Vase, 183
grog, 54
Guggenheim Museum, 12
Gulden, Tyler, 236, 237

H

Hamada, Shōji, 46, 66
Hardy, Anne, 213
Heatter, Maida, 169
Hernández de Toledo, Francisco,
  134
honey, *161*
  honey-peach preserves, 165
honeybees, *134,* 186
  beekeeping, 161, *161, 163*
Hopkins, David, 241
House & Garden, 10, 152, *152*
Huang Fei, *64*
Huh, Young, 46
Humboldt, Alexander von, 134–35
humor, 101
Humpty Dumpty, 50, 54

I

inner voice, 225
inspiration
  for ceramics, 46–49
  for garden, 140
irises, *140, 148, 203*

J

Jacobs, Chad, *183*
Japanese pottery, *49,* 69
Javits Convention Center gift show,
  241

Jingdezhen, China, 64, *64*
Johnson, Linda Lee, 95
Johnson, Philip, *183*
journals, *46*

K

Kent, William, 140
Kiefer, Anselm, *85*
kilns, 38, *42,* 49, 57, 66, 106–9,
  236–37, *236, 237*
  pyrometric cones in, 66
kintsugi, 10
knitwear, 24, 119, 183
KRB, 241

L

laughter, 101
Lauder, Aerin, *23, 183*
leek and goat cheese tart, 30
Linnaeus, Carl, 134
Lloyd, Christopher, 120, 140

M

Mackenzie, Warren, 69
Maida Heatter's New Book of Great
  Desserts (Heatter), 169
Martin, Agnes, 12
McCormick, Charlie, 127, 183
Merrick, Amy, 186
Metropolitan Museum of Art, 23,
  46, 54, *92,* 241
Meyerowitz, Joel, 214
Mieke ten Have, *183*
minestrone, 235
molds, 116, *116*
  flower, 156, *158*

Morandi, Giorgio, 214, *214*
morning, 110
Morris, Cedric, *140*
mugs, 10, *19*
muscari, *147, 229*
Museum of the Alhambra, *37*

N

narcissi, *144, 229*
Neue Galerie, *183*
New York Botanical Garden, 124, 140
New York Times, 98, 110
Niagara Ceramics, 183
notebooks, *46*

O

Ohr, George, 46, *87*
Omega Workshops, 24, 25, 50, *88*
open studios, 180, *180*
oribe glaze, 67, *73*
Orr, Stephen, 152
oxblood glaze, 66, 67–69, *70, 74*

P

Palmer, Wally, 24, 105, 120, 173, 180, 183, 210
pasta, fresh, 61–63
peach-honey preserves, 165
Penn, Irving, 214, *223*
peonies, *148, 200, 205*
perseverance, 29
photographic principles, 216
    contrast, *218*
    light, *216*
    point of view, *223*
    warm versus cool, *221*
photography, 210, *210,* 213, 214, *214*
Picasso, Pablo, 46
pie dough, 29
    goat cheese and leek tart, 30
    tarte tatin, 98
Piercy, Marge, 19
Plain English, 213
Pleydell-Bouverie, Katherine, 69
Pope, Sandra and Nori, 140
poppies, *147, 193, 194, 200*
porcelain, 37, *37,* 38, *38,* 50, *50,* 57, *57, 58,* 64, 87
potato-stamp prints, 170, *170*
pot chop, 170, *170*
pots, finishing touches for, 78
    beading, *82*
    drawing and painting, *88*
    fluting, *87*
    handles, *78*
    holes, *85*
    pedestals, *80*
    ruffles, *85*
    sculptural gestures, *87*
pottery and ceramics, 10–12, 17, 25, 241
    aesthetics and purpose in, 19
    bisque firing in, 38, *42,* 50
    building a pot, step-by-step, 90
    business promotion and, 34–35
    Chinese, 46–49, 64, 67, 69, *97,* 241
    Cycladic, *23,* 46, 54, *78, 88*
    documentation of, 179, 210, *210,* 213, 214, *214,* 216
    earthenware, *25,* 37, 38, 50–54, *50, 52, 58,* 241
    equipment for, 112–15
    Etruscan, *46,* 54, *78*
    flower casts for, 156, *158*
    glazes for, *see* glazes
    happy accidents in, 152
    inspiration for, 46–49
    Japanese, *49,* 69
    kilns for, 38, *42,* 49, 57, 66, 106–9, 236–37, *236, 237*
    making a pot, 37–38
    and memory of clay, 37
    molds for, 116, *116*
    packing and shipping of, 111, *177*
    and personality of clay, 50
    porcelain, 37, *37,* 38, *38,* 50, *50,* 57, *57, 58,* 64, 87
    pricing work, 95
    pyrometric cones and, 66
    terra-cotta, 37, 38, 50, *50,* 54–55, *54*
    throwing a pot, centering clay for, 32
    throwing a pot, step-by-step, 76
    wheels for, 106, 109
Pottery Workshop, 64
pricing work, 95
Pritchard, Imogen, 213
purpose, 19, 32
pyrometric cones, 66

Q

qigong, 101

R

randomness, 152
recipes
    almond cake, 226
    date-nut bread, 169
    fresh pasta, 61–63

goat cheese and leek tart, 30
honey–peach preserves, 165
minestrone, 235
perfect roast chicken, 174
roasted tomato sauce, 151
tarte tatin, 98
repetition, 96–97
Richards, M. C., 32
Rie, Lucie, 46
Rodin, Auguste, 46
roses, *190, 193, 200*
Rothman, Sabine, 76

S

Sackville-West, Vita, 140
Sakonnet Garden, 186
Schrager, Victor, 161
self-care, 232
self-reliance, 45
Shakers, *57, 109*
shino glaze, *68,* 69
Silvermine Arts Center, 25
social media, 213, *213*
Sōetsu, Yanagi, 13, 19

Spry, Constance, 190
Steichen, Edward, 214
Stein, Gertrude, 119
stoneware, *25*
studio, 105, 106–9
    open studios, 180, *180*
    work schedule in, 110–11

T

Takashimaya, 35, 111
tarts
    goat cheese and leek tart, 30
    tarte tatin, 98
terra-cotta, 37, 38, 50, *50,* 54–55, *54*
Thompson, Emily, 183, *183*
time, 119
"To Be of Use" (Piercy),
    19
Tolstoy, Leo, 45
tomato sauce, 151
Tortu, Christian, 35
tulipieres, 46, *52,* 54
tulips, *144, 193, 194, 200, 205,
    206, 229*

V

Vogue, 214

W

Wagner, David, 210
Waters, Alice, 30
Wave Hill, 140
website, 213
well-being, 232
Wedgwood, Josiah, 50
Weems, Carrie Mae, 97
woodstove, *109*
working at home, 105
    parenting and, 170
    see also studio
working row by row, 119

Y

You've Got Mail, 95